Praise for
of David

"David Deida must have the biggest balls in c̲...̲ ̲...̲r̲y̲ spirituality."
> — Vijay Rana, The Watkins Review

"As a woman, I've never felt so understood and validated."
> —Marci Shimoff, Co-Author of
> *Chicken Soup for the Woman's Soul*

*"The openness, the love! What lively new language David Deida finds for
the unsayable!"*
> —Coleman Barks, Author of *The Essential Rumi*

*"Every once in a while, someone comes along whose work is clearly a next step. Their
ideas seem to answer some collective question hanging out in the culture. Their books
and seminars become an underground buzz, and within a period of time, their ideas
become part of our cultural vernacular. David Deida is such a person. In a time not
too far off from now, his ideas will have spread like wildfire."*
> —Marianne Williamson, Author of *A Return to Love*

*"There are few categories I know of for an original like David Deida; for his teachings
there is no pigeonhole. He is a bridge-builder between East and West, between ancient
and modern wisdom traditions. David is in the dynamic living oral tradition of
maverick spiritual teachers who, like free-jazz musicians, can riff directly on Reality,
outside of established forms. Mark my words: in a future that I hope is not too far
off, David Deida's original western Dharma will be widely known as one of the most
sublime and accessible expressions of the essence of spiritual practice that is freely
offered today."*
> —Lama Surya Das, Author of *Awakening the Buddha Within*

*"David Deida's teachings on this central human concern, sexuality, emanate from a
deeply trustworthy source. He has undergone his own rigorous training and practice,
which manifests in precise, gentle, and thorough teachings. Like Zen, the fruition of
David's work is openness, compassion, and love."*
> —Genpo Roshi, Author of *The Eye Never Sleeps*

"David Deida's work reveals a depth of loving the human condition and understanding its immanent spirituality I've seldom seen, even in a glimmer. It's hard for me to find words with which to express my appreciation and admiration for this unique gift."

—Jenny Wade, PhD, Author of *Changes of Mind*

"David Deida brings spirituality down from the clouds and back into our bodies where it belongs. His no-nonsense approach to refining our spiritual sensibilities comes as a welcome intervention to both New Age and conservative trends in contemporary spirituality. Deida helps us to get REAL in a world where reality is an increasingly rare commodity."

—Mariana Caplan, Author of *Halfway Up the Mountain: The Error of Premature Claims to Enlightenment*

"I feel that Deida has reached a new level of poetic genius in his writing, and his understanding of feminine psychology astounds me."

—Miranda Shaw, PhD, Author of *Passionate Enlightenment: Women in Tantric Buddhism*

"The Way of the Superior Man *is a bold and challenging and very perceptive book. The cutting-edge masculinity of these pages is sexually strong and spiritually clear…. Deida challenges and instructs men to live on their edge, to go forth uncompromisingly in search of their own deepest truths and greatest purpose. He pulls no punches and brooks no weakness."*

—*NAPRA Review*

"With uncommon honesty and unparalleled insight into the deepest desires of the masculine heart, Deida explores the most challenging and important issues in men's lives. Covering everything from work and career, to dealing with sex, women, and love, to finding purpose in an increasingly superficial and mechanical world, The Way of the Superior Man *reveals how a man can live a life of fulfillment without compromise by relaxing into the truth of his very being, discovering his deepest vision, and giving his gifts without holding anything back. What emerges is a wholly revolutionary look at what it means to be a man in today's world as well as an astonishingly practical guidebook to living a masculine life of integrity, authenticity, and freedom."*

—*The Midwest Book Review*, Reviewer's Choice

the WAY of the SUPERIOR MAN

Also by David Deida

BOOKS

Dear Lover
A Woman's Guide to Men, Sex, and Love's Deepest Bliss

Blue Truth
A Spiritual Guide to Life & Death and Love & Sex

Intimate Communion
Awakening Your Sexual Essence

Finding God Through Sex
Awakening the One of Spirit Through the Two of Flesh

Wild Nights
Conversations with Mykonos about Passionate Love, Extraordinary Sex, and How to Open to God

The Enlightened Sex Manual
Sexual Skills for the Superior Lover

It's a Guy Thing
An Owner's Manual for Women

Instant Enlightenment
Fast, Deep, and Sexy

AUDIO

Enlightened Sex
Finding Freedom & Fullness through Sexual Union

The Teaching Sessions:
The Way of the Superior Man
Revolutionary Tools and Essential Exercises for Mastering the Challenges of Women, Work, and Sexual Desire

WEB SITE

www.deida.info

the WAY *of the* SUPERIOR MAN

A Spiritual Guide to Mastering the Challenges of
Women, Work, and Sexual Desire

David Deida

SOUNDS TRUE
Boulder, Colorado

Important Caution

Please read this

Although anyone may find the practices, disciplines, and understandings in this book
to be useful, it is made available with the understanding that neither the author nor
the publisher are engaged in presenting specific medical, psychological, emotional,
sexual, or spiritual advice. Nor is anything in this book intended to be a diagnosis,
prescription, recommendation, or cure for any specific kind of medical, psychological,
emotional, sexual, or spiritual problem. Each person has unique needs and this book
cannot take these individual differences into account. Each person should engage
in a program of treatment, prevention, cure, or general health only in consultation
with a licensed, qualified physician, therapist, or other competent professional. Any
person suffering from venereal disease or any local illness of his or her sexual organs
or prostate gland should consult a medical doctor and a qualified instructor of sexual
yoga before practicing the sexual methods described in this book.

Sounds True, Inc., Boulder, CO 80306

© 1997, 2004 David Deida

Sounds True is a trademark of Sounds True, Inc. All rights reserved. No part
of this book may be reproduced in any form or by any means, electronic or
mechanical, including photocopying, recording, or by any information storage and
retrieval system, without permission in writing from the author and publisher.

Published 2004
Printed in Canada

ISBN 978-1-59179-257-4

Library of Congress Control Number: 2004115454

25 24

With deepest gratitude,
To the intimate partners and teachers
Who have drenched my life with their love and wisdom

Table of Contents

PART THREE: Working With Polarity and Energy

PART FOUR: What Women Really Want

PART FIVE: Your Dark Side

PART SIX: Feminine Attractiveness

May this book serve the liberation of your true gifts, so that countless multitudes of beings may benefit even more from your living and loving.

Preface

My publisher asked me to write a preface to this new edition of *The Way of the Superior Man*.

Originally, I wrote this book as a practical guide for men and their intimate lovers. I wanted to share with readers the lessons I had learned in life—specifically, how a man can grow spiritually while passionately tussling with the challenges of women, work, and sexual desire.

Now, years later, after sharing this work with thousands of men and women, straight and gay, single and coupled, I can confirm that the lessons presented in these chapters really produce results. And in today's world of rapid sexual and spiritual evolution—and thus confusion—these lessons may be more relevant than ever.

One of the more important lessons is this: as evolving human beings, we can learn that mastery is an important phase to accomplish and pass through in this school of life where we are learning to love more artfully.

Through the way described in this book, I have learned to love a woman into light, earn as much money as I want doing what I love to do, and master the arts of sexual loving. You can, too.

And then you will open to your next lessons, made possible by your real growth, just as you have achieved and outgrown all of your interests up until now.

What you loved as a child is less interesting to you now as an adult. And what occupies your attention now will cease to sooner or later. This growth is both natural and good. We are designed to outgrow everything—including our desire to experience and improve the realms of money, sex, and intimacy.

The Way of the Superior Man shows you how a man and his lover can learn the lessons necessary to grow to the next step—where the mind opens as feeling and the body is only light. There is a way to grow through these lessons, too, I'm told, but first things first.

Live completely. Know your deepest purpose. Give the gift you were born to give. Enjoy sex as a cosmic portal into love's wonders. Serve your friends so they may grow. And, through the inevitable cycles of breathtaking success and gut wrenching despair, when you have mastered and outgrown the challenges of women, work, and sexual desire, be willing to forget you were ever born.

Eventually—and I'm telling you in advance, just like I was told—the way of the superior man renders obsolete everything that can be known or experienced.

For now, start with what concerns you. I did. What my teachers and life required that I grow to understand—the path that worked for me as a man in a world of infinite possibilities—is offered in the chapters of this book. You will lay down your own path as you grow beyond your need to experience or know anything at all.

So, here's my summation for a new preface: Stop waiting. Feel everything. Love achingly. Give impeccably. Let go.

Repeat with whatever remains, as long as you are moved to do so.

This way dissolves wide open. ◆

Introduction

This book is a guide for a specific kind of newly evolving man. This man is unabashedly masculine—he is purposeful, confident, and directed, living his chosen way of life with deep integrity and humor—and he is sensitive, spontaneous, and spiritually alive, with a heart-commitment to discovering and living his deepest truth.

This kind of man is totally turned on by the feminine. He loves to take his woman sexually, to ravish her, but not in some old-style macho fashion. Rather, he wants to ravish her with so much love she is vanished, they both vanish, in the fullness of loving itself. He is dedicated to incarnating love on this earth, through his work and his sexuality, and he does so as a free man, bound neither by outer convention nor inner cowardice.

This newly evolving man is not a scared bully, posturing like some King Kong in charge of the universe. Nor is he a new age wimp, all spineless, smiley, and starry-eyed. He has embraced both his inner masculine and feminine, and he no longer holds onto either of them. He doesn't need to be right all the time, nor does he need to be always safe, cooperative, and sharing, like an androgynous Mr. Nice Guy. He simply lives from his deepest core, fearlessly giving his gifts, feeling through the fleeting moment into the openness of existence, totally committed to magnifying love.

To help illuminate the purpose of *The Way of the Superior Man*, I will draw on a few principles of sexuality and spiritual growth which are developed in my book *Intimate Communion*.*

* David Deida, 1995. *Intimate Communion*. Deerfield Beach, Florida: Health Communications, Inc.

Until fairly recently, modern roles for men and women were fixed and separated. Men were supposed to go out and earn money. Women were supposed to stay home and take care of the kids. Men often manipulated their women through physical and financial dominance and threat. Women often manipulated their men through emotional and sexual strokes and stabs. The typical and extreme caricatures of this previous time are the macho jerk and the submissive housewife. If you are reading this book, you have probably outgrown this first stage of sexual identity. Or at least you can smile about it.

Next came (and is still coming) a stage in which men and women both sought to balance their inner masculine and feminine energies toward "50/50," becoming more like one another. For instance, in the United States in the 1960s, men began to emphasize their inner feminine. They learned to go with the flow. They let go of their rigid, one-dimensional masculine stance and embraced long hair, colorful clothes, nature, music, and a more carefree and sensual lifestyle, all means of embellishing or magnifying radiance, energy, and the abundant force of life—magnifying the feminine.

Meanwhile, many women were doing just the opposite. They were magnifying their inner masculine, which, at the level of human character, appears as direction, or clarity of purpose, and vision. Women gained financial and political independence. They strengthened their careers, focused more on personal long term goals, went to school in increasing numbers for advanced degrees, and learned to be more assertive in their needs and desires.

Chances are, if you are reading this book, you are more balanced than your parents were. If you are a woman, you are probably more independent and assertive than your mother was. If you are a man, you are probably more emotionally expressive and open-minded than your father was. Or, at least such qualities seem acceptable to you, even if you don't express them yourself. Remember, not that many years ago, a man who got his hair styled or a woman who wore a business suit was often considered suspect.

It was a good thing, as time progressed, for men to embrace their inner feminine and women to embrace their inner masculine. They became less fragmented and more whole in the process. They became less dependent on each other: men could, indeed, change diapers, and women were completely capable of emptying the mouse traps. Macho men became more loose and feeling. Submissive housewives became more independent and directed. In terms of social roles, men and women became more similar. This was an improvement for everyone.

But this 50/50 stage is only a second and intermediate stage of growth for men and women, not an endpoint. Side effects of this trend toward sexual similarity can be seen as a major cause of today's unhappiness in intimacy. The trend toward 50/50 has resulted in economic and social equality, but also in sexual neutrality. Bank accounts are balancing while passions are fizzling out. Men are less macho while sex and violence continue to increase on TV and in the movies. Women are more in control of their economic destiny while they go in increasing numbers to therapists and doctors to cope with stress related dis-ease. Why is this happening?

In my workshops and consultations I hear independent and successful women complaining that many of today's men have become "wimps," too weak and ambiguous to really trust. Sensitive and affectionate men are complaining that many of today's women have become "ballbusters," too hardened and emotionally guarded to fully embrace. Is this the ultimate expression of human sexual wisdom and evolution, or is there another step to take?

To answer these questions, we need to understand the nature of sexual passion and spiritual openness. Sexual attraction is based on sexual polarity, which is the force of passion that arcs between masculine and feminine poles. All natural forces flow between two poles. The North and South Poles of the Earth create a force of magnetism. The positive and negative poles of your electrical outlet or car battery create an electrical flow. In the same way, masculine and feminine poles between people create the flow of sexual feeling. This is sexual polarity.

This force of attraction, which flows between the two different poles of masculine and feminine, is the dynamism that often disappears in modern relationships. If you want real passion, you need a ravisher and a ravishee; otherwise, you just have two buddies who decide to rub genitals in bed.

Each of us, man or woman, possesses both inner masculine and inner feminine qualities. Men can wear earrings, tenderly hug each other, and dance ecstatically in the woods. Women can change the oil in the car, accumulate political and financial power, and box in the ring. Men can take care of their children. Women can fight for their country. We have proven these things. Just about anyone can animate either masculine or feminine energy in any particular moment. (Although they still might have a strong preference to do one or the other, which we will get to in a moment.)

The bottom line of today's newly emerging 50/50, or "second stage," relationship is this: If men and women are clinging to a politically correct sameness even in moments of intimacy, then sexual attraction disappears. I don't mean just the desire for intercourse, but the juice of the entire relationship begins to dry up. The love may still be strong, the friendship may still be strong, but the sexual polarity fades, unless *in moments of intimacy* one partner is willing to play the masculine pole and one partner is willing to play the feminine. You have to animate the masculine and feminine differences if you want to play in the field of sexual passion.

This is true in homosexual as well as heterosexual relationships. Actually, the gay and lesbian community is acutely aware that sexual polarity is independent of gender. But you still need two poles for a passionate play of sexuality to persist in a relationship: masculine and feminine, top and bottom, butch and femme—whatever you want to call these reciprocal poles of sexual play.

It is up to you: You can have a loving friendship between two similars, but you need a more masculine and a more feminine partner in the moments when you want strong sexual polarity.

It doesn't matter if both partners are men or both are women. It doesn't matter if, in a heterosexual relationship, the man plays the feminine pole and the woman plays the masculine pole. It doesn't matter if you change every day who plays the masculine pole and who plays the feminine pole. For sexual polarity, you need an energetic polarity, an attractive difference between masculine and feminine. *You don't need this difference for love, but you do need it for ongoing sexual passion.*

For some people who have what I call a more balanced sexual essence, sexual polarity doesn't really matter. They don't really *want* much passion in intimacy. They don't want a loving tussle full of sexual inspiration and innuendo. They would rather have a civilized friendship full of love and human sharing without the passionate ups and downs. And for these people, this book will be irrelevant, possibly even offensive.

This book is written specifically for people who have a more masculine sexual essence, and their lovers, who will have a more feminine sexual essence—since you always attract your sexual reciprocal. These people can't help but be attracted into relationships based on difference, for better or for worse.

Your sexual essence is your sexual core. If you have a more masculine sexual essence, you would, of course, enjoy staying home and playing with the kids, but deep down, you are driven by a sense of mission. You may not know your mission, but unless you discover this deep purpose and live it fully, your life will feel empty at its core, even if your intimate relationship and family life are full of love.

If you have a more feminine sexual essence, your professional life may be incredibly successful, but your core won't be fulfilled unless love is flowing fully in your family or intimate life.

The "mission" or the search for freedom is the priority of the masculine, whereas the search for love is the priority of the feminine. This is why people with masculine essences would rather watch a football game or boxing match on TV than a love story. Sports are all about achieving freedom, such as by breaking free of your opponent's tackle or barrage of punches, and about succeeding at your mission, by carrying the ball into the end zone or remaining standing after 10 rounds. For the masculine, mission, competition, and putting it all on the line (indeed, facing death), are all forms of ecstasy. Witness the masculine popularity of war stories, dangerous heroism, and sports playoffs.

But, for the feminine, the search for love touches the core. Whether on soap operas, in love stories, or talking with friends about relationships, the desire for love is what appears in feminine forms of entertainment.

The feminine wants to be filled with love, and if the bliss of real love is not forthcoming, chocolate and ice cream—or a good romantic drama—will do. The masculine wants to feel the bliss of a life lived at the edge, and if he doesn't have the balls to do it himself, he'll watch it on TV, in sporting events and cop shows.

Even happy and fulfilled men and women find it enjoyable to watch sports and eat ice cream, of course. I am just trying to make a point: Even though all people have both masculine and feminine qualities that they could use in any moment—to kick corporate ass or nurture children, for instance—most men and women also have a more masculine or feminine core. And this shows up in their regularly chosen entertainments, as much as in their preferred sexual play.

Think about it. Would you rather that your sexual partner was physically stronger than you, or would you prefer to feel your lover's physical vulnerability? Which would turn you on more, to pin your partner on the bed below you or to be pinned below your partner? To be swept off your feet by a sensitive and strong lover or to feel your lover surrender, swooning in your arms? You may want both at different times, but most often which turns you on more?

Or, does each of these alternatives turn you on just the same? That is, are you just as turned on by a sexual partner who is physically weaker than you as by one who is stronger, or exactly the same strength?

Most people, about 90% in my experience, seem to have a definite preference. They definitely either prefer that their partner kills the cockroach crawling toward them, or they're fine with doing the crunchy job themselves, perhaps with sporting fervor. Most people clearly favor watching a romantic love story on TV to a bloody boxing match, or vice versa. They might be able to enjoy both at times, but their core becomes more emotionally involved in one or the other. If you have ever seen a group of masculine people watching a Super Bowl game, you know just how emotional the masculine core becomes while beholding a good mission of people living at their edge and giving their gifts—or getting slaughtered for failing.

So, about 90% of people have either a more masculine or a more feminine sexual essence. Passionately, lovingly, and fiercely, they would like to be ravished by, or to ravish, their intimate partner, at least some of the time, in addition to having a loving friendship. This holds true for homosexual and heterosexual people alike.

About 10% of people, men and women, heterosexual and homosexual, have a more balanced essence. Boxing matches and love stories equally make them emotional, or not. It doesn't really matter to them whether their lover is physically stronger or more vulnerable than them. Sexual polarity just isn't that important to them in relationships anyway.

Regardless of gender or sexual orientation, if you want to experience deep spiritual and sexual fulfillment, you must know your natural sexual essence—masculine, feminine, or balanced—and live true to it. You can't deny your true sexual essence by covering it with layers of false energy for years, and then expect to know your authentic purpose and be free in the flow of love. This book is a guide to shedding pretense and living true to your core, specifically for people who have a masculine sexual essence and their feminine essenced lovers who have to deal with them.

In a well-intentioned effort to provide equal opportunity and rights for men and women, many people are inadvertently squashing their true sexual essence. They don't have to; it's certainly possible to provide equality while also living true to your masculine or feminine core. But most people don't. So they suffer.

Most people are forgetting that the sameness that works in the office does not work in intimacy for about 90% of couples: those couples composed of partners with masculine and feminine essences rather than balanced essences. If sexual passion is to flow in these polarized intimacies, masculine and feminine differences should be magnified, not diminished, in moments of intimacy. When these polarities are lessened due to family and work obligations, sexual attraction is diminished, along with spiritual depth and physical health.

Stressing your masculine or feminine essence into a falsely balanced persona affects virtually every part of you. Many people with true feminine essences manifest a whole range of disturbed physiological symptoms as their feminine energy "dries up" due to running excess masculine energy through their body, year after year, in order to fit into the masculine style of work. And many people with masculine essences, seeking to fit in with the feminine style of cooperation and energy flow, disconnect from their sense of life purpose and inhibit their deep truth, afraid of the consequences of being authentic to their own masculine core. Hence, the frequent complaints about too many ballbusters and wimps.

Furthermore, when you deny your true core you deny the possibility of true and real love. Love is openness, through and through. And true spirituality is the practice of love, the practice of openness. A person who denies their own essence and hides their true desires is divided and unable to relax into the full openness of love. Their spirit becomes cramped and kinked. Unable to feel the natural ease and unconstrained power of their own core, they feel threatened and frightened. This fear is the texture of their inability to open fully in love. Such a person is spiritually handicapped, obstructed at heart, even though they may have achieved a safe relationship and a successful career.

So, as a culture, we have advanced in terms of personal freedom, sexual equality, and social rights, but we have remained spiritually thwarted and afraid. For the sake of individual autonomy and social fairness, with only good intentions in mind, we have erroneously begun to deny, smooth out, and neutralize our masculine and feminine differences. In doing so, people often end up denying their deepest core desires, which are rooted in their true sexual essence. A lot of people today *think* they have a balanced sexual essence, but in most cases they are actually suppressing the natural desires which spring from their real masculine or feminine core.

It is important to admit what is real if you are going to really deal with your life. *The Way of the Superior Man* focuses on many of these issues which we often sidestep or deny. For example, if you truly have a balanced sexual essence, then you are just not that sexually distracted by anyone. But if you are, for instance, a heterosexual man with a true masculine sexual essence, then you will be more or less constantly sexually attracted to feminine women you see all day, at the workplace and on the street. To married women as well as teenage girls. As long as they shine the feminine light, you will feel the pull. How do you turn this potential sexual problem into a spiritual gift?

If you have a masculine sexual essence then you would probably admit, if you were being brutally honest, that your intimate relationship is just not as important to you as the "mission" in your life—but you still want a full and energetic intimate relationship, perhaps quite badly. How do you deal with this often misunderstood dilemma?

To answer questions such as these as clearly as possible, I have chosen to write this book as if speaking to the most common case of a masculine sexual essence: a heterosexual man with a masculine sexual essence. As I've said, there are many other possible arrangements of gender, essence, and sexual preference. You could, for instance, be a heterosexual woman with a masculine essence married to a man with a feminine essence, or a homosexual man with a masculine essence married to a man with a feminine essence, and the principles in this book would still apply to you. But I trust the reader to make the appropriate adjustment in wording for his or her own unique case if it is different from this most common one.

I suppose the book could have been called, "The Way of the Superior Person With a Masculine Essence," but the whole thing would become unwieldy if I tried to unfold every possible permutation of "he" and "she" and "masculine sexual essence" and "balanced sexual essence" and "feminine sexual essence" in every possible heterosexual, bisexual and homosexual relationship. In the end, I opted for simplicity. You can add the permutations yourself. If you or your partner has a masculine sexual essence—regardless of anatomy, gender, or sexual preference—this book will help you clarify your life and enable you to give your deepest gifts, personally and at work, sexually and spiritually.

The Way of the Superior Man is a book written explicitly for people who have already achieved respect for other genders and sexual preferences, and who consider men and women to be social, economic, and political equals. Now, we are ready to move to the next stage, grounded in this mutual respect and equality, but celebrating the sexual and spiritual passions inherent in the masculine/feminine polarity.

It is time to evolve beyond the macho jerk ideal, all spine and no heart. It is also time to evolve beyond the sensitive and caring wimp ideal, all heart and no spine. Heart and spine must be united in a single man, and then gone beyond in the fullest expression of love and consciousness possible, which requires a deep relaxation into the infinite openness of this present moment. And this takes a new kind of guts. This is *The Way of the Superior Man.* ◆

PART

ONE

A Man's
Way

1
Stop Hoping for a Completion of Anything in Life

Most men make the error of thinking that one day it will be done. They think, "If I can work enough, then one day I could rest." Or, "One day my woman will understand something and then she will stop complaining." Or, "I'm only doing this now so that one day I can do what I really want with my life." The masculine error is to think that eventually things will be different in some fundamental way. They won't. It never ends. As long as life continues, the creative challenge is to tussle, play, and make love with the present moment while giving your unique gift.

It's never going to be over, so stop waiting for the good stuff. As of now, spend a minimum of one hour a day doing whatever you are waiting to do until your finances are more secure, or until the children have grown and left home, or until you have finished your obligations and you feel free to do what you really want to do. Don't wait any longer. Don't believe in the myth of "one day when everything will be different." Do what you love to do, what you are waiting to do, what you've been born to do, now.

Spend at least one hour a day doing whatever you simply love to do—what you deeply feel you need to do, in your heart—in spite of the daily duties that seem to constrain you. However, be forewarned: you may discover that you don't, or can't, do it; that in fact, your fantasy of your future life is simply a fantasy.

Most postponements are excuses for a lack of creative discipline. Limited money and family obligations have never stopped a man who *really* wanted to do something, although they provide excuses for a man who is not really up to the creative challenge in the first place. Find out today whether you are willing to do what it takes to give your gift fully. As a first step, spend at least an hour today giving your fullest gift, whatever that is for today, so that when you go to sleep at night you know you couldn't have lived your day with more courage, creativity, and giving.

In addition to the myth that one day your life will be fundamentally different, you may believe, and hope, that one day your woman will be fundamentally different. Don't wait. Assume she's going to be however she is, forever. If your woman's behavior or mood is truly intolerable to you, you should leave her, and don't look back (since you cannot change her). However, if you find her behavior or mood is merely distasteful or a hassle, realize that she will always seem this way: The feminine always seems chaotic and complicated from the perspective of the masculine.

The next time you notice yourself trying to fix your woman so that she will no longer _____ (fill in the blank), relax and give her love by touching her and telling her that you love her when she is this way (whatever you filled in the blank with). Embrace her, or wrestle with her, or scream and yell for the heck of it, but make no effort to bring an end to that which pisses you off. Practice love instead of trying to bring an end to the quality that bothers you. You can't escape the tussle with the feminine. Learn to find humor in the unending emotional drama the feminine seems to enjoy so much. The love that you magnify may realign her behavior, but your effort to fix her and your frustration never will.

The world and your woman will always present you with unforeseen challenges. You are either living fully, giving your gift in the midst of those challenges, even today, or you are waiting for an imaginary future which will never come. Men who have lived significant lives are men who never waited: not for money, security, ease, or women. Feel what you want to give most as a gift, to your woman and to the world, and do what you can to give it today. Every moment waited is a moment wasted, and each wasted moment degrades your clarity of purpose. ◆

2

Live With an Open Heart Even If It Hurts

....

Closing down in the midst of pain is a denial
of a man's true nature. A superior man is free in
feeling and action, even amidst great pain and
hurt. If necessary, a man should live with a
hurting heart rather than a closed one. He should
learn to stay in the wound of pain and act with
spontaneous skill and love even from that place.

Imagine failing at a major project, lying to your woman and getting
caught, or overhearing her joke about your shortcomings in bed. How
do you react with your body, breath, and eyes? Notice if you react to a
person or situation that hurts you by withdrawing, hiding, or closing in on
yourself. Notice if there are times when you find it difficult to look into
someone's eyes, or times your chest and solar plexus become tense and
contracted. These are signs of an unskillful reaction to hurt. Contracted
and closed in on yourself, you are unable to act. You are trapped in your
own self-protective tension, no longer a free man.

The superior man practices opening during these times of automatic
closure. Open the front of your body so your chest and solar plexus are
not tense. Sit or stand up straight and full, opening the front of your body,
softening your chest and belly, wide and free. Breathe down through your
chest and solar plexus, deep into your belly. Look directly into the eyes
of whomever you are with, feeling your own pain as well as feeling the

other person. Only when the front of your body is relaxed and opened, your breath full and deep, and your gaze unguarded and directly connected with another person's eyes, can your fullest intelligence manifest spontaneously in the situation. To act as a superior man, a samurai of relationship, you must feel the entire situation with your whole body. A closed body is unable to sense subtle cues and signals, and therefore unable to act with mastery in the situation. ◆

3
Live As If Your Father Were Dead

A man must love his father and yet be free of his father's expectations and criticisms in order to be a free man.

Imagine that your father has died, or remember when he did die. Are there any feelings of relief associated with his death? Now that he is dead, is any part of you happy that you need not live up to his expectations or suffer his criticisms?

How would you have lived your life differently if you had never tried to please your father? If you never tried to show your father that you were worthy? If you never felt burdened by your father's critical eye?

For the next three days, do at least one activity a day that you have avoided or suppressed because of the influence of your father. In this way, practice being free of his subtle expectations, which may now reside within your own self-judgment. Practice being free in this way, once each day for three days, even if you still feel fearful, limited, unworthy, or burdened by your father's expectations ◆

4
Know Your Real Edge and Don't Fake It

It is honorable for a man to admit his fears, resistance,
and edge of practice. It is simply true that each man
has his limit, his capacity for growth, and his destiny.
But it is dishonorable for him to lie to himself or others
about his real place. He shouldn't pretend he is more
enlightened than he is—nor should he stop short of his
actual edge. The more a man is playing his real edge,
the more valuable he is as good company for other
men, the more he can be trusted to be authentic and
fully present. Where a man's edge is located is less
important than whether he is actually living his edge in
truth, rather than being lazy or deluded.

Pick an area of your life: perhaps your intimate relationship, your career, your relationship with your children, or your spiritual practice. For instance, you are currently doing something to earn a living. Where do your fears stop you from making a larger contribution to mankind, from earning a higher income, or from earning money in a more creative and enjoyable way? If you were absolutely fearless, would you be earning a living in exactly the same way as you are now? Your edge is where you stop short, or where you compromise your fullest gift, and, instead, cater to your fears.

Have you lost touch with the fears that are limiting and shaping your income and style of livelihood? If you have deluded yourself and feel that you are not afraid, then you are lying to yourself. All men are afraid, unless they are perfectly free. If you cannot admit this, you are pretending to yourself, and to others. Your friends will feel your fear, even if you do not. Thus, they will lose trust in you, knowing you are deluding yourself, lying to yourself, and are therefore likely to lie to them, consciously or unconsciously.

Or, perhaps you are very aware of your fears: your fear to take risks, your fear of failing, or your fear of succeeding. Perhaps you are comfortable with your life, and you fear the lifestyle change that might accompany a change in career, even though the new career will be closer to what you really want to do with your life. Some men fear the feeling of fear and therefore don't even approach their edge. They choose a job they know they can do well and easily, and don't even approach the fullest giving of their gift. Their lives are relatively secure and comfortable, but dead. They lack the aliveness, the depth, and the inspirational energy that is the sign of a man living at his edge. If you are this kind of man who is hanging back, working hard perhaps, but not at your real edge, other men will not be able to trust that you can and will help them live at their edge and give their fullest gift.

As an experiment, describe your edge with respect to your career out loud to yourself. Say something like, "I know I could be earning more money, but I am too lazy to put in the extra hours it would take. I know that I could give more of my true gift, but I am afraid that I may not succeed, and then I will be a penniless failure. I've spent 15 years developing my career, and I'm afraid to let go of it and start fresh, even though I know that I spend most of my life doing things I have no real interest in doing. I could be making money in more creative ways, but I spend too much time watching TV rather than being creative."

Honor your edge. Honor your choices. Be honest with yourself about them. Be honest with your friends about them. A fearful man who knows he is fearful is far more trustable than a fearful man who isn't aware of his fear. And a fearful man who still leans into his fear, living at his edge and putting his gift out from there, is more trustworthy and more inspirational than a fearful man who hangs back in the comfort zone, unwilling to even experience his fear on a day to day level. A free man is free to acknowledge his fears, without hiding them, or hiding from them. Live with your lips pressed against your fears, kissing your fears, neither pulling back nor aggressively violating them. ◆

5

Always Hold To
Your Deepest Realization

*Eternity must be a man's home, moment by
moment. Without it, he is lost, always striving,
grasping at puffs of smoke. A man must do
anything necessary to glimpse, and then stabilize, this
ever-fresh realization, and organize his life around it.*

Make your life an ongoing process of being who you are, at your deepest, most easeful levels of being. Everything other than this process
is secondary. Your job, your children, your wife, your money, your artistic
creations, your pleasures—they are all superficial and empty, if they are not
floating in the deep sea of your conscious loving. How many hours today was
your attention focused in the realm of changes—on events, people, thoughts,
and experiences—and how often was your attention relaxed into its source?
Where is your attention right now? Can you feel its source? Even for a moment, can you feel that which makes attention conscious and aware? Can
you feel the deepest nature of attention? What happens when you simply,
effortlessly, allow attention to subside into its source?

This source is never changing and always present. It is the constant,
silent tone behind and pervading the music of life. Feel into this source as
deeply as possible, and then re-approach your work, intimacy, family, and
creative efforts. When you make money, make money from this source.
Find out what happens to the details of your life when you live more consistently from this source.

Use aids to support your relaxation into, and creation from, this source. Read books that remind you of who you are, in truth. Spend time with people who inspire and reflect the source to you. Meditate, contemplate, or pray daily so that you steep yourself in the source.

If you are like most men, you have strong habits that rivet your attention to the events and tasks of the day. Days and nights fly by for years, and life slips through your fingers, your attention absorbed in the seeming world of necessary responsibilities. But all of it is empty if we do not live our responsibilities as expressions of our depth of being and heart-truth.

Know eternity. Do whatever it takes. And from this depth of being, live the details of your life. But if you postpone the process of submerging yourself in the source for the sake of taking care of business first, your life will be spent in hours and days of business, and then it will be gone. Only if you are well grounded in that which is larger than life will you be able to play life with humor, knowing that each task is a mirage of necessity.

Even if you find yourself in some trivial moment, watching TV or cleaning up a mess in the kitchen, feel the truth of who you are. Feel the boundless cognizance in which each instant seems and vanishes. All moments are the same intensity of clarity, completeness, and humor when you meet each moment with your deepest realization. Nothing that has ever happened has made any difference to the One who you are. ◆

6

Never Change Your Mind Just to Please a Woman

*If a woman suggests something that changes a man's
perspective, then he should make a new decision
based on his new perspective. But he should never
betray his own deepest knowledge and intuition in
order to please his woman or "go along" with her.
Both she and he will be weakened by such an action.
They will grow to resent each other, and the crust of
accumulated inauthenticity will burden their love, as
well as their capacity for free action.*

You should always listen to your woman, and then make your own decision. If you choose to go with your woman's suggestion even when deep in your heart you feel that another decision is more wise, you are, in effect, saying, "I don't trust my own wisdom." You are weakening yourself by telling yourself this. You are weakening your woman's trust in you: why should she trust your wisdom if you don't?

When you deny your deep truth to please your woman, everyone will feel your lack of authenticity. They will sense that your false smile hides an inner division. Your friends, children, and business colleagues may love you, but they won't trust you, since you don't trust your own core intent. And, more importantly, your own sense of inauthenticity will burden your capacity to act with clarity. Your actions won't jibe with your core.

However, if you listen to your woman, taking everything she says into account and making your own best decision, then you are acting in accordance with your core. You are saying, in effect, "My deepest wisdom is leading me to this decision. If I am wrong, I will learn from it, and my wisdom will have deepened. I'm willing to be wrong, and grow from it. I trust this process of acting from my deepest wisdom."

This attitude of self-trust engenders others' trust in you. You may be wrong, but you are willing to find out, and thus grow from the experience. You are open to listening to others, but in the end, you will take the responsibility for making your own decision. There is nobody else to blame.

However, if you give up your real decision to follow your woman's, then you will blame her for being wrong if she is wrong, and you will feel disempowered if she is right, having denied yourself the opportunity to act from your core and grow from your mistakes. Be open to changing your feeling based on whatever your woman might reveal to you—through her words or her body language—and then make your own decision, based on your deepest intuitive wisdom and knowledge. You may make the right decision or the wrong one, but whatever happens, it is your best shot, and you will strengthen your capacity for future action. ◆

7

Your Purpose Must Come Before Your Relationship

Every man knows that his highest purpose in life
cannot be reduced to any particular relationship.
If a man prioritizes his relationship over his highest
purpose, he weakens himself, disserves the universe,
and cheats his woman of an authentic man who
can offer her full, undivided presence.

Admit to yourself that if you had to choose one or the other, the perfect intimate relationship or achieving your highest purpose in life, you would choose to succeed at your purpose. Just this self-knowledge often relieves much pressure a man feels to prioritize his relationship when, in fact, it is not his highest priority.

Your mission is your priority. Unless you know your mission and have aligned your life to it, your core will feel empty. Your presence in the world will be weakened, as will your presence with your intimate partner. The next time you notice yourself "giving in" to your woman, postponing your mission and denying your true purpose in order to spend time with her, stop. Tell your woman that you love her, but you cannot deny your heart's purpose. Tell her that you will spend 30 minutes (or some specific time) with her in absolute attention and total presence, but then you must return to carry on your mission.

Your woman will be more fulfilled with 30 minutes a day of undivided attention and ravishing love than she will with a few hours of your weak and divided presence when your heart really isn't into it. Time you spend with your woman should be time you really want to be with her more than anything else. If you'd rather be doing something else, she'll feel it. Both of you will be dissatisfied. ◆

8

Lean Just Beyond Your Edge

In any given moment, a man's growth is optimized
if he leans just beyond his edge, his capacity, his
fear. He should not be too lazy, happily stagnating
in the zone of security and comfort. Nor should
he push far beyond his edge, stressing himself
unnecessarily, unable to metabolize his experience.
He should lean just slightly beyond the edge of fear
and discomfort. Constantly. In everything he does.

Once you are honest with yourself about your real edge, it is best to lean just beyond it. Very few men have the guts for this practice. Most men either settle for the easy path or self-aggrandize themselves by taking the extreme hard path. Your insecurity may cause you to doubt yourself, and so you take the easy way, not even approaching your real edge or your real gift. Alternatively, your insecurity may lead you to push, push, push, seeking to become victorious over your own sense of lack.

Both approaches avoid your actual condition in the moment, which is often fear. If you are stressfully avoiding your fear, you cannot relax into the fearless.

Your fear is the sharpest definition of your self. You should know it. You should feel it virtually constantly. Fear needs to become your friend, so that you are no longer uncomfortable with it. Rather, primary fear shows you that you are at your edge. Staying with the fear, staying at your edge, allows real transformation to occur. Neither lazy nor aggressive, playing your edge allows you to perceive the moment with the least amount of distortion. You are willing to be with what is, rather than trying to escape it by pulling back from it, or trying to escape it by pushing beyond it into some future goal.

Fear of fear may lead you to hang back, living a lesser life than you are capable. Fear of fear may lead you to push ahead, living a false life, off-center, tense and missing the moment. But the capacity to feel this moment, including your fear, without trying to escape it, creates a state of alive and humble spontaneity. You are ready for the unknown as it unfolds, since you are not pulled back or pushed forward from the horizon of the moment. You are hanging right over the edge.

By leaning just beyond your fear, you challenge your limits compassionately, without trying to escape the feeling of fear itself. You step beyond the solid ground of security with an open heart. You stand in the space of unknowingness, raw and awake. Here, the gravity of deep being will attend you to the only place where fear is obsolete: the eternal free fall of home. Where you always are.

Own your fear, and lean just beyond it. In every aspect of your life. Starting now. ◆

9
Do It
for Love

*The way a man penetrates the world should
be the same way he penetrates his woman: not
merely for personal gain or pleasure, but to
magnify love, openness, and depth.*

The next time you embrace your woman sexually, feel your ultimate desire. Your deepest desire in life. Feel why you are doing anything at all in life, and, specifically, why you are uniting with your lover. There may be many lesser reasons, but what is your deepest, ultimate reason?

Most men's ultimate reason for doing anything has to do with discovering their deepest truth, enjoying total freedom and love, and giving their fullest gifts.

Yet, many men settle for enjoying a little bit of freedom and love while incompletely giving their gifts. They enjoy the freedom to buy a nice car, to have loving sex fairly often, and to sleep late on Sunday. They generously donate their spare cash to a good cause, lovingly buy their woman a diamond ring, and happily coach a little league team. These are enjoyable freedoms and real gifts that make a significant difference in people's lives. But, for many men, it is still not enough.

The freedom or love they have achieved and the way they have given their gifts often leave a sense of incompleteness. Something is still lacking. There is still a desire to go beyond, to untrap themselves, to enjoy life free of a subtle sense of constraint, loneliness, underlying tension, and fear. And, for many men, try as they might, the sense remains that their fullest gift remains ungiven. Their life feels somewhat false at its core, as does their sexing.

When a man gives his true gift of sex to his woman, he penetrates and blooms her beyond all limits into love. It is the same with the world. To bloom woman and world for real takes authenticity, persistence, and courage of heart. A man must know the truth at his core and be willing to give his gifts fully. No holding back. He must be willing to dedicate his sex and his life to magnifying love by penetrating woman and world with his true gifts. This willingness is rare.

Many men are willing to poke their woman and bloom her in a mediocre way, sharing a few orgasms and a few emotional moments of bonding before going over tomorrow's schedule. Many men are willing to poke the world and bloom it in a mediocre way, making a few bucks and contributing enough betterment so they don't feel like their life is a total waste.

But very few men are willing to do the deed for real, to use everything they've got to liberate their woman and the world into the deepest possible truth, love, and openness. Few men are willing to give their deepest genius, their true endowment, the poetry of their very being, with every thrust of sex and life. Most men are limpened with doubts and uncertainties. Or they hold back their true drive because of fear. So they diddle their woman and the world just enough to extract the pleasure and comfort they need to assuage their nagging sense of falsity and incompleteness.

But if you are willing to discover and embrace your truth, lean through your fears, and give everything you've got, you can penetrate the world and your woman from the core of your being and bloom them into love without limit. You can ravish your woman so deeply that her surrender breaks your heart into light. You can press yourself into the world with such enduring love that the world opens and receives your deepest gifts.

There is no essential difference between entering your woman's feminine heart and entering fully into the world. Both forms of intercourse, sexual and worldly, require sensitivity, spontaneity, and a strong connection to deep truth in order to penetrate chaos and closure in a way that love prevails.

Neither woman nor world are predictable. They will often seem to resist your gifts and test your capacity to persist. And, just as surely, they will tenderly respond to the authenticity of your relaxed ministrations, the freedom expressed in your humor, and the invasion of your adamant love. They will open in love and receive you fully—only to resist and test you again, moments or days later. Neither woman nor world can be second-guessed, or fooled. They know when you are just dicking around. They want to receive you for real.

There are two ways to deal with woman and world without compromising your true gifts or dribbling away the force of your deep being. One way is to renounce sexual intimacy and worldliness, totally dedicating yourself without distraction or compromise to the path you choose to pursue, free of the seemingly constant demands of woman and world.

The other way is to "fuck" both to smithereens, to ravish them with your love unsheathed, to give your true gifts despite the constant tussle of woman and world, to smelt your authentic gifts in this friction of opposition and surrender, to thrust love from the freedom of your deep being even as your body and mind die blissfully through a crucifixion of inevitable pleasure and pain, attraction and repulsion, gain and loss. No gifts left ungiven. No limit to the depth of being. Only openness, freedom, and love as the legacy of your intercourse with woman and world.

If you are going to tryst with women and world at all, better to go all the way and ravish them from the depths of your true core, blooming them open with the wide gifts of your unrelenting heart. Otherwise, if you sheepishly penetrate them to gratify your own needs, your woman and the world will feel your lack of dedication, depth, and truth. Rather than yielding in love to your loving, they will distract you, suck your energy, and draw you into endless complications, so that your life and relationship become an almost constant search for release from constraint.

You can be a renunciate and live alone, apart from woman and world. But if you choose a life of sexual and worldly intercourse, you will feel trapped by woman and world unless you are free in the midst of "true fuck," yielding yourself into the giving, holding nothing back, dissolving all time in the open of love. Through thick and thin, this is the way of the superior man. ◆

10

Enjoy Your Friends' Criticism

A man's capacity to receive another man's direct criticism is a measure of his capacity to receive masculine energy. If he doesn't have a good relationship to masculine energy (e.g., his father), then he will act like a woman and be hurt or defensive rather than make use of other men's criticism.

About once a week, you should sit down with your closest men friends and discuss what you are doing in your life and what you are afraid of doing. The conversation should be short and simple. You should state where you are at. Then, your friends should give you a behavioral experiment, something you can do that will reveal something to you, or grant more freedom in your life.

"I want to have an affair with Denise, but I don't want to hurt my wife. I'm afraid of her finding out," you might say.

"You've been talking about Denise now for six months. You are wasting your life energy on this fantasy. You should either have sex with her by tomorrow night, or drop the whole thing and never talk about it again," your friends might say, challenging your hesitation and mediocrity.

"OK. I know I'm not going to do it. I see now that I am too afraid of ruining my marriage to have an affair with Denise. My marriage is more important than my desire for Denise. I'll drop it and refocus on the priorities in my life. Thanks."

Your close men friends should be willing to challenge your mediocrity by suggesting a concrete action you can perform that will pop you out of your rut, one way or the other. And you must be willing to offer them your brutal honesty, in the same way, if you are all to grow. Good friends should not tolerate mediocrity in one another. If you are at your edge, your men friends should respect that, but not let you off the hook. They should honor your fears, and, in love, continue to goad you beyond them, without pushing you.

If you merely want support from your men friends without challenge, it bespeaks an unresolved issue you may have with your father, whether he is alive or dead. The father force is the force of loving challenge and guidance. Without this masculine force in your life, your direction becomes unchecked, and you are liable to meander in the mush of your own ambiguity and indecision. Your close men friends can provide the stark light of love—uncompromised by a fearful Mr. Nice act—by which you can see the direction you really want to go.

Choose men friends who themselves are living at their edge, facing their fears and living just beyond them. Men of this kind can love you without protecting you from the necessary confrontation with reality that your life involves. You should be able to trust that these friends will tell you about your life as they see it, offer you a specific action which will shed light on your own position, and give you the support necessary to live in the freedom just beyond your edge, which is not always, or even usually, comfortable. ◆

11

If You Don't Know Your Purpose, Discover It, Now

Without a conscious life-purpose a man is totally lost, drifting, adapting to events rather than creating events. Without knowing his life-purpose a man lives a weakened, impotent existence, perhaps eventually becoming even sexually impotent, or prone to mechanical and disinterested sex.

▼

The core of your life is your purpose. Everything in your life, from your diet to your career, must be aligned with your purpose if you are to act with coherence and integrity in the world. If you know your purpose, your deepest desire, then the secret of success is to discipline your life so that you support your deepest purpose and minimize distractions and detours.

But if you don't know your deepest desire, then you can't align your life to it. Everything in your life is dissociated from your core. You go to work, but since it's not connected to your deepest purpose, it is just a job, a way to earn money. You go through your daily round with your family and friends, but each moment is just another in a long string of moments, going nowhere, not inherently profound.

Disconnected from your core, you feel weak. This empty feeling will undermine not only your "erection" in the world, but your erection with your woman, too.

However, when you know your true purpose, which is your core desire in life, each moment can become a full expression of your core desire.

Every instant of career, every instant of intimacy, is filled with the power of your heart purpose. You are no longer just going through the motions at work and with your woman, but you are living the truth of your life, and giving the gifts of your love, moment by moment. Such a life is complete unto itself in every instant.

The superior man is not seeking for fulfillment through work and woman, because he is already full. For him, work and intimacy are opportunities to give his gifts, and be vanished in the bliss of the giving. ◆

12

Be Willing To Change
Everything in Your Life

*A man must be prepared to give 100% to his purpose,
fulfill his karma or dissolve it, and then let go of that
specific form of living. He must be capable of not
knowing what to do with his life, entering a period of
unknowingness and waiting for a vision or a new form
of purpose to emerge. These cycles of strong specific
action followed by periods of not knowing what the
hell is going on are natural for a man who is shedding
layers of karma in his relaxation into truth.*

As you open yourself to living at your edge, your deepest purpose
will slowly begin to make itself known. In the meantime, you will
experience layer after layer of purposes, each one getting closer and closer
to the fullness of your deepest purpose. It is as if your deepest purpose is
at the center of your being, and it is surrounded by layers of concentric
circles, each circle being a lesser purpose. Your life consists of penetrating
each circle, from the outside toward the center.

The outer purposes are often the purposes you have inherited or
learned from your parents and your childhood experiences. Perhaps your
father was a fireman, so you wanted to be a fireman. Or, in reaction to
him, you've decided to be an arsonist. In any case, the outer circles, the
purposes you often apply yourself to early in life, are most likely only
distant approximations of your deepest purpose.

If your deepest purpose is to meditate and realize God, you might find that before you can totally dedicate yourself to this practice you must work your way through the concentric circles of playing with sexual partners, using drugs, getting married, raising children, developing a career, and finally, having dissolved your fascination and need to do all of that, getting down to the business of full-time meditation.

As you dissolve each layer and move toward the center, you will more and more be living from your deeper purposes, and then your deepest heart purpose, whatever that is, in every moment. However, you probably are not living your deepest purpose yet. You probably need to burn off the karma, or fulfill the need, of the present purpose by which you are fascinated and distracted.

It's easy to feel disappointed by life; success is never as fulfilling as you think it is going to be. But there is a reason for this. Successfully completing a lesser purpose doesn't feel very good for very long, because it is simply preparation for advancing toward a greater embodiment of your deeper purpose. Each purpose, each mission, is meant to be fully lived to the point where it becomes empty, boring, and useless. Then it should be discarded. This is a sign of growth, but you may mistake it for a sign of failure.

For instance, you may take on a business project, work at it for several years, and then suddenly find yourself totally disinterested. You know that if you stayed with it for another few years you would reap much greater financial reward than if you left the project now. But the project no longer calls you. You no longer feel interested in the project. You have developed skills over the last few years working on the project, but it hasn't yet come to fruition. You may wonder, now that you have the skills, should you stick with it and bring the project to fruition, even though the work feels empty to you?

Well, maybe you should stick with it. Maybe you are bailing out too soon, afraid of success or failure, or just too lazy to persevere. This is one possibility. Ask your close men friends if they feel you are simply losing steam, wimping out, or afraid to bring your project to completion. If they feel you are bailing out too soon, stick with it.

However, there is also the possibility that you have completed your karma in this area. It is possible that this was one layer of purpose, which you have now fulfilled, on the way to another layer of purpose, closer to your deepest purpose.

Among the signs of fulfilling or completing a layer of purpose are these:

1. You suddenly have no interest whatsoever in a project or mission that, just previously, motivated you highly.
2. You feel surprisingly free of any regrets whatsoever, for starting the project or for ending it.
3. Even though you may not have the slightest idea of what you are going to do next, you feel clear, unconfused, and, especially, unburdened.
4. You feel an increase in energy at the prospect of ceasing your involvement with the project.
5. The project seems almost silly, like collecting shoelaces or wallpapering your house with gas station receipts. Sure, you could do it, but why would you want to?

If you experience these signs, it is probably time to stop working on this project. You must end your involvement impeccably, however, making sure there are no loose ends and that you do not burden anybody's life by stopping your involvement. This might take some time, but it is important that this layer of your purpose ends cleanly and does not create any new karma, or obligation, that will burden you or others in the future.

The next layer of your unfolding purpose may make itself clear immediately. More often, however, it does not. After completing one layer of purpose, you might not know what to do with your life. You know that the old project is over for you, but you are not sure of what is next. At this point, you must wait for a vision.

There is no way to rush this process. You may need to get an intermediary job to hold you over until the next layer of purpose makes itself clear. Or, perhaps you have enough money to simply wait. But in any case, it is important to open yourself to a vision of what is next. You stay open to a vision of your deeper purpose by not filling your time with distractions. Don't watch TV or play computer games. Don't go out drinking beer with your friends every night or start dating a bunch of women. Simply wait. You may wish to go on a retreat in a remote area and be by yourself. Whatever it is you decide to do, consciously keep yourself open and available to receiving a vision of what is next. It will come.

When it comes, it usually won't be a detailed vision. You will probably have a sense of what direction to move in, but the practical steps might not make themselves clear. When the impulse begins to arise, act on it. Don't wait for the details. Learn by trial and error what it is you are to do.

For instance, perhaps you were a stockbroker and then finished that particular layer of purpose. You saved up some money, so now you are waiting for a vision of your next layer. After three weeks of going crazy, not knowing what you are going to do with your life, you begin to feel that you want to work with people. You begin to fantasize about using your financial skills to help people set up their own businesses. You have a few friends who have great intentions to save the world, but they are lousy businessmen and can't seem to get off the ground. So you call them and offer your help.

As you help them, you continually feel for the "groove" of your purpose. You might have a few false starts. But, eventually, you find that dozens of non-profit groups are telephoning you, asking for your advice. It feels as if the universe is supporting you in this direction. You have no idea whether you can earn a living doing this, but it feels right for now. So you apply yourself fully to it. You give your gift 100%, without holding anything back.

Soon, a wealthy man finds out about what you are doing. He admires your total commitment and your orientation to serve others. He becomes your patron. Now, you are set. You have a good income, you are doing what you really want to do, and you are helping others. You love what you do, so you generate love in those who come in contact with you. Your life feels full.

And then, one day, a few years later, it is finished. This layer has dissolved. And the cycle begins again, and again, until you have penetrated all the layers into your deepest purpose. Then, you act fully, until that purpose, too, is dissolved in the bliss of the love that you are. ◆

13
Don't Use Your Family As an Excuse

If a man never discovers his deepest purpose, or if he
permanently compromises it and uses his family as an
excuse for doing so, then his core becomes weakened
and he loses depth and presence. His woman loses
trust and sexual polarity with him, even though he
may be putting much energy into parenting their
children and doing the housework. A man should, of
course, be a full participant in caring for children and
the household. But if he gives up his deepest purpose
to do so, ultimately, everyone suffers.

Take care of the children and the house as much as you want. Just remember that if you give up your true purpose to do so for too long, you are not really helping anyone.

Parenting children, as well as any responsible commitment in love, requires that you transcend your own personal preferences for the sake of the larger commitment, for the sake of service in love. This is a natural part of being a householder. However, you cannot abnegate your deepest purpose to do so, or else you will feel frustrated, eventually resigning yourself to a lesser life than you know you are capable of living.

This self-resignation will communicate itself to your woman and your children. They will feel your weakness. Your woman will begin to take charge more than she really wants, since you are clearly not capable of taking charge yourself, and someone has to do it. Your children will challenge your capacity to discipline them, since they can feel your own lack of authentic self-discipline. Try as you might, once you have negated your own deep purpose, your household will become a place where everybody tests your capacity to stand your ground, and you will lose.

Obviously, as a father or a householder, you will want to give your love, skill, energy, and time to your family. It will be your joy, and it will also be a necessity. However, the motive to dedicate time to householding may or may not be symmetrical between partners, and this should be an ongoing discovery for each couple. This motive may change over time for both men and women as their lives grow through different stages.

The priority of the feminine, in men and women, is the flow of love in relationship. The priority of the masculine, in men and women, is the mission which leads to freedom. Ultimately, true freedom and true love are the same. However, the journey of the masculine and feminine to this unity of love and freedom is very different.

If your woman has a more feminine essence than you, or if she is in a more feminine phase of life than you, then her priority will be the flow of love in her life: her core will be much more fulfilled by the love she shares with the children than yours will be. You will also feel great fulfillment sharing love with your children, but if you have a masculine core, or if you are in a masculine phase of your life, this fulfillment will not touch your deepest parts in the same way. Even if you love your children every bit as much as your woman does, your relationship with them will only be part of your deepest life purpose.

What is your deepest life purpose? For some men, their deepest life purpose is their family. If you are one of these men, then you probably aren't concerned about the issue of whether or not you are using your family as an excuse. Many men, however, regardless of how much they love their family, also feel a deeper calling. If they do not live true to this calling, then their core weakens, even if they genuinely love and desire to serve their family.

When you know your direction and are living it fully, your core is alive and strong. Your children will naturally feel this. They will respond to your clarity and presence differently than they will respond to your ambiguity—an ambiguity that results from having detoured from your deepest purpose because you think it's "right" or "fair" that you spend time with them. A short period of time with a father who is absolutely present, full in love, undivided inside, and sure of his mission in life, will affect your children much more positively than if they spend lots of time with a father who is ambiguous in his intent and has lost touch with his deepest purpose, no matter how much he loves his children.

Children learn most from their parents by osmosis. If their father is subtly weakened and compromised, this will flavor their experience of his love. Just as you did with your father, your children will unconsciously replicate or react to the emotional taste they absorb from you. Your essential emotional tone—at ease in your deepest purpose or fearful in the ambiguity of your intent—becomes part of your children's home.

If you and your woman both work, it is better to make arrangements with other families to "timeshare" childcaring, or to hire someone to help with your children, than to permanently compromise your deepest purpose and truth because you feel you must do so to spend more time with your children. It is not the amount of time but the quality of the interaction that most influences a child's growth. Children are exquisitely sensitive to emotional tone. If you are not full in your core, aligned with your deepest purpose and living a life of authentic commitment, your children will feel it.

For their sake, your sake, and your woman's sake, discover your deepest purpose, commit yourself completely to its process, and find a way to embrace your family as you do so. Be with your woman and your children without compromise or ambiguity. Don't use your family as an excuse to be less than you can be. With birth control so readily available, children are a choice. If you choose to be a householder and raise children, you are responsible for serving them with as much authentic love as possible, which you can only give if your life is aligned with your deepest purpose.

Don't cheat your family of your fullest core, and don't use them as an excuse to avoid the work it will take to manifest your highest vision. You can give love to your family and engage your life's work, if you discipline yourself to act on your deepest desires with priority. Then, when you are with your family, you are with them totally, since there is no chronically unfinished business in your life to distract you, and no inner ambiguity about where you want to be or what you really want to be doing. ◆

14

Don't Get Lost in Tasks and Duties

Whatever the specifics of a man's purpose, he must always refresh the transcendental element of his life through regular meditation and retreat. A man should never get lost in the details of his life and forget that, ultimately and in truth, life amounts to nothing other than what is the deepest truth of this present moment. Tasks don't get a man anywhere more conscious or free than he is capable of being in this present moment.

You have probably noticed yourself in the "do mode." You are totally focused, intent on getting a task done. You don't want to be disturbed. If anyone tries to interrupt you with a question, you ignore them, or give them a quick answer so you can keep on track. This "do mode" is very common among men. Whether you are trying to hear something on TV or finish a report by midnight, your attention is focused on the task at hand and you don't want to be distracted.

This "do mode" is one of men's biggest strengths and weaknesses. It's great to be able to plow through obstructions and get the job done. And it's good to keep yourself disciplined and on purpose. But if you forget your larger purpose while pursuing the small and endless tasks of daily life, then you have reduced yourself to a machine of picayune.

Even now, as you read this, you may be in a "do mode," totally ensconced in the process of reading. If you were to die right now, what would be the feeling texture of your last moment? Are you feeling the infinite mystery of existence, so that your last moment would be one of awe and gratitude? Is your heart so wide open that your last moment would dissolve in perfect love? Or, are you so absorbed in some task that you would hardly notice death upon you, until the last instant, whoosh, and everything is gone?

The test of your fullness in every moment is your capacity to die in free and loving surrender, knowing you've done everything you could do while alive to give your gift and know the truth of being. Have you loved fully? Or, do you have unexpressed feelings that would taint your last moment with regret? Do you consistently relax into the awe of immense mystery? Or, are you so absorbed in your work and projects that you no longer feel the miracle of existence, each moment emerging from and dissolving into the great unknowable? Has your task addiction built blinders that limit the vastness of your vision, even now?

Tasks are important, but no amount of duties adds up to love, freedom, or full consciousness. You cannot do enough, nor can you do the right things, so that you will finally feel complete. Doing is simply the nature of your bodily life. If you want the body to continue, you must eat and breathe. You must work, care for your family, and brush your teeth. But these are just the mechanics of life on Earth. They never come to the absolute truth of your being.

When you do your tasks in the right way, they liberate your life energy so that you can attend to what really matters—the investigation, realization, and embodiment of true freedom. Do you even know what this means? Have you devoted yourself to finding out the deepest truth of your own existence? If, in this very moment, your tasks are not supporting your life in this way, you must drop them or change them so that they do. Otherwise, you are wasting your life.

Whereas many women waste precious time swirling in emotional currents and eddies, many men waste their birth seeking the completion of tasks. Nose to the grindstone, day after day, year after year, and you become a robot of duty. Rather, raise your eyes, see to the horizon, and do your tasks in the spirit of sweeping out your house on a sunny day.

To help you remember the triviality of your daily tasks, interrupt your schedule with refreshers. These refreshers should cut to your core and strip the fat off the moment. Consider your own death. Behold an image of the most enlightened being you know. Contemplate the mystery of existence. Relax into the deepest and most profound loving of which you are capable. In your own way, remember the infinite, and then return to the task at hand. This way, you will never lose perspective and begin to think that life is a matter of tasks. You are not a drone. You are the unbounded mystery of love. Be so, without forgetting your tasks. ◆

15

Stop Hoping for Your Woman to Get Easier

A woman often seems to test her man's capacity to remain unperturbed in his truth and purpose. She tests him to feel his freedom and depth of love, to know that he is trustable. Her tests may come in the form of complaining, challenging him, changing her mind, doubting him, distracting him, or even undermining his purpose in a subtle or not so subtle way. A man should never think his woman's testing is going to end and his life will get easier. Rather, he should appreciate that she does these things to feel his strength, integrity, and openness. Her desire is for his deepest truth and love. As he grows, so will her testing.

▼

Every moment of your life is either a test or a celebration. The same is true about every moment with your woman, only doubly so. Not only is her simple existence a test for you, but one of her deepest pleasures in intimacy is testing you, and then feeling you are not moved off course by her challenge.

The most erotic moment for a woman is feeling that you are Shiva, the divine masculine: unperturbable, totally loving, fully present, and all-pervading. She cannot move you, because you already are what you are, with or without her. She cannot scare you away, because you already penetrate her in fearless love, pervading her heart and body. She cannot distract you, because your one-pointed commitment to truth will not bend to her wiles. Feeling this hugeness of love and freedom in you, she can trust you, utterly, and surrender her testing in celebration of love.

Until she wants to feel you as Shiva again. And then the testing will begin anew. In fact, it is precisely when you are most Shiva-like that she will most test you.

Perhaps you have been working toward some financial goal, and finally you have succeeded. After months or years of effort, you have creatively earned a large amount of money. You feel happy, full, successful. You feel great. You come home to your woman and want to share the news with her.

"I just made a million dollars today."

"That's nice."

"That's nice!!?? You know how hard I've been working for this."

"I know. It feels like I haven't seen you in months. Did you remember to pick up the milk on the way home?"

"Oh, sorry. I forgot. But who cares? We could buy a dairy farm now!"

"I asked you to pick up the milk three times this morning, and I put a note on your briefcase. How could you forget?"

"I said I'm sorry. Look, I'll go get the damn milk..."

Why is she being this way? Because she simply wants to deflate your success? No. She is challenging you because your success doesn't mean shit to her, unless you are free and loving. And if you are free and loving, nothing she says can collapse you. She wants to feel you are uncollapsable, so she pokes you in your weak spot.

Of course she knows how much this moment of success means to you. This is precisely why she is negating it. Not because she wants to hurt you. But because she wants to feel Shiva. She wants to feel your strength. She wants to feel that your happiness is not dependent on her response, nor on you making a million dollars. She wants to feel you are a superior man.

It's a tall order to be this free, and in your more mediocre moments you will wish your woman would settle for less. But if you are a man who is living his fullest, willing to play his edge and grow through difficulties, then you will want her to test you. You may not *like* it. But you don't want her to settle for some bozo who depends on his woman's response to be happy. If you are aligned with your mission, you are essentially happy, even though times cycle between difficult and easy. You don't need your woman's strokes to fulfill your mission. It still feels good when she strokes you, but you don't need mommy anymore, telling you what a good boy you are. And your woman doesn't want you to need mommy. In fact, it sickens her.

If your woman is weak, she may settle for a weak man, and therefore play into your need to feel like a good boy. But if she is a good woman, a strong woman, she won't tolerate your childish needs for a pat on the head, collecting bigger toys, and being king of the mountain. A good woman will love the childlike part of you, but she wants your life to be guided by your deepest truths, not your untended childhood wounds. She wants to feel that at your core you have grown beyond the need for kudos and million-dollar toys. She wants to feel your self-generated strength of truth.

So she will test you. She might not be fully conscious of why she is doing it, but she will poke your weak spots, especially in moments of your superficial success, in order to feel your strength. If you collapse, you've flunked the test. You have let your woman deflate you. You have demonstrated your dependence on her for external validation. Even if you just made a million dollars, you are a weak man. Your woman cannot trust you fully.

If you remain full and strong, humorous and happy, your truth unperturbed by her testing, then you pass the test.

"Honey, I'll get you some milk, all right," you say as you sweep her off the ground and lay her on the couch, laughing, kissing, looking deeply into her eyes, and "milking" her happiness with the confident loving of your caresses.

She can relax and trust your Shiva core. She can surrender the tensions around her heart. You are trustable. You don't need her validation in order for you to be loving. You simply *are* loving. The truth of you is love. Your fullness is independent of mommy. You are not only a man, you are a superior man: a man who does his best to live as love in the world and in his intimacy, a man whose heart remains open and whose truth remains strong even when his woman criticizes him, a man who can find the humor in forgetting to pick up the milk on a day he made a million dollars.

This is the kind of man your woman can trust. Now, the moment is a moment of celebration. Now, she can relax and truly join in your jubilation, knowing you are not dependent on her praise for your happiness. It will last, perhaps, ten minutes. And then she will test you again.

It never ends. A woman will always test her man for the pleasure of feeling his strength in loving, his capacity to transcend nuisance, his persistence in his own truth, and his capacity to share that truth in love with her, even when she is complaining—*especially* when she is complaining. Her complaint is the beginning of her pleasure. It is not true criticism, but a test of your Shiva-hood. The criticism is entirely dissolved in love as soon as she feels your humor and happiness in the midst of the poke.

It never ends. This is the secret. You can't get out of it. Finding a different woman won't get you out of it. Therapy won't get you out of it. Financial or sexual mastery won't get you out of it. Your woman is testing you because she loves you. She wants to feel your truth. She wants to feel your love. And she wants to feel that your truth and love are stronger than the barbs she can throw at you. Then she can relax and surrender into the polarity of man and woman. Then she can trust you.

The most loving women are the women who will test you the most. She wants you to be your fullest, most magnificent self. She won't settle for anything less. She knows it is true of you. She knows in your deepest heart you are free, you are Shiva. Anything less than that she will torment. And, as you know, she's quite good at it.

Yet, if your purpose is to be free, you wouldn't have it any other way. ◆

PART

TWO

Dealing With
Women

16

Women Are
Not Liars

"Keeping your word" is a masculine trait, in men or
women. A person with a feminine essence may not
keep her word, yet it is not exactly "lying." In the
feminine reality, words and facts take a second
place to emotions and the shifting moods of
relationship. When she says, "I hate you," or "I'll
never move to Texas," or "I don't want to go to the
movies," it is often more a reflection of a transient
feeling-wave than a well considered stance with
respect to events and experience. On the other hand,
the masculine means what it says. A man's word
is his honor. The feminine says what it feels. A
woman's word is her true expression in the moment.

When you listen to your woman, listen to her as you would the ocean, or the wind in the leaves. The sounds you hear from her are sounds of the motion of her feeling-energy. Of course, there are times when she speaks in the masculine style of meaning exactly what she says, but more often, and almost always in emotional moments, what she says is the sound of her feelings. Her feminine speech is far more like poetry than like a clearcut agenda for action. In an emotional moment, what she says she is going to do is actually an expression of what she feels like doing in the moment. Her feelings, and therefore what she is actually going to do, could change in five minutes. It could change every five minutes.

Whenever you are surprised by your woman's actions, and you say to her, "But you said…," you are forgetting that she has a feminine essence. What your woman says is like a cloud passing in the sky: well-formed, coherent, and unrecognizable moments later. The cloud is an expression of the precise physics of water, wind, and air. Your woman's words are expressions of the physics of her feelings, your relationship, and the nuances of the present situation, seen and unseen. A moment later, these factors will change, and so will your woman's expressions.

You might ask her, "Do you want to go to the movies?"

She might reply, "Not really."

Then you hug her and spin her around and say, "Let's go to the movies!"

And she says, "OK!"

She is not talking about her desire to go to the movies. She is talking about the feeling of your relationship in the present moment. If after she said she didn't want to go to the movies, you said fine and sat down to watch TV, you would be missing the point. She is not really saying she doesn't want to go to the movies, even though that is what she's saying.

This is not lying. For a man, or for anyone speaking in the masculine style, to say something that is not true is lying. But, for the feminine, truth is a thin concept compared to the thickness of her flow of feelings. The "truth" of the feminine is whatever she is really feeling, *in this present moment*.

So, when she says that she wants to move to Pittsburgh with you, and then, after you have sold the house, she says she doesn't want to move with you, don't start yelling, "But you said…!" When she first told you she wanted to move, she was feeling good about the relationship. When she then told you she doesn't want to move, she was feeling bad about the relationship. Instead of arguing about what she said or didn't say, establish love in the intimacy first.

The basic rule is this: Don't believe the literal content of what your woman says unless love is flowing deeply and fully in the moment when she says it. And even then, know that she is probably talking about her current feelings, not necessarily about the subject of whatever she is talking about. Never base your plans on what a woman says she wants to do, unless she is in the full flow of love when she says it. And then, expect her to change her mind at any moment when her feelings change. Remember that a woman's feelings may be more sensitive to an unseen realm of nature than are yours. Try to differentiate between your woman's shifting moods and her sensitive wisdom.

Women are not liars, although they often seem that way to men. This is why a man must ultimately be responsible for making his own decisions, based on the deepest truth he can fathom. Otherwise, if he bends his course of truth to compromise for his woman's current and changing expressions, he will probably end up blaming her.

You should hear what your woman has to say and feel her depth carefully. Then, after you have fully considered her input, make your best possible decision from your own deep core. This way, if your woman subsequently changes her mind, you won't resent her for compromising your path. Rather, you can enjoy her subtle sensitivity and changing emotional weather patterns. You can proceed with or modify your actions in full gear, knowing you are always making the best choice available to you, having taken her depth of wisdom—and her fluctuations of expression and mood—wholly into account. ◆

17
Praise
Her

The masculine grows by challenge, but the feminine grows by praise. A man must be unabashed and expressed in his appreciation for his woman. Praise her freely.

Men grow by challenge. As a boy, other boys would challenge you in order to inspire you: "I bet you can't jump over that fence." In a place like boot camp, you are told you are a worthless slimedog, and this kind of insult challenges you to be your best. So, as a man, you probably have a masculine habit of challenging people, including your woman, in order to get her to improve or grow.

Only the masculine side of your woman will grow through challenge. The feminine side thrives on support and praise. Telling her, "I love the shape of your body," will be much greater incentive for her to exercise than telling her, "I hope you don't gain any more weight."

Praise always magnifies the quality of your woman that you praise. "You're so beautiful when you smile," is much more effective than, "You're so ugly when you frown," although they both indicate your desire for her smile. When speaking to your woman, it is always better to call the glass half full than half empty.

Praise is literal food for feminine qualities. If you want your woman to grow in her radiance, health, happiness, love, beauty, power, and depth, praise these qualities. Praise them daily, a number of times.

It is a difficult practice for most men to learn, but you must learn to praise the very qualities you feel are not yet praiseworthy in order for them to become so. In other words, praise the tiny quality that you want to grow. If you know that your woman would be healthier if she exercised more, don't tell her that. It will feel like an insult to her, a rejection of her the way she is. Instead, tell her how sexy she is when she sweats in her leotards. Tell her how much it turns you on when she moves her body. Whatever parts of her body you really like, let her know, frequently.

Praising the things you really enjoy when she exercises will magnify her exercising. On the other hand, by telling her why she should exercise, you are indicating that she is not acceptable to you the way she is. Praise works. Information doesn't. Praise motivates. Challenge doesn't. Try it. Praise specific things you love about your woman 5 to 10 times a day. Find out what happens. ◆

18

Tolerating Her Leads
to Resenting Her

*A man gets resentful and frustrated with his woman
when he is too afraid, weak, or unskilled to penetrate
her moods and tests into love. He wishes she were easier
to deal with. But it is not entirely her fault that she is
bitchy and complaining. It is also a reflection of her lack
of being penetrated by love. When a man resigns, and
simply tolerates his woman's self-destructive moods, it
is a sign of his weakness. His attitude has become one
of wanting to escape women and the world, rather than
wanting to serve women and the world into love. A man
shouldn't tolerate bitchy and complaining moodiness in
his woman, but he should serve her and love her with
every ounce of his skill and perseverance. Then, if she
cannot or will not open in love, he might decide to end his
relationship with her, harboring no anger or resentment,
because he knows he has done everything he could.*

The whole point of an intimacy is to serve each other in growth and
love, hopefully in better ways than we can serve ourselves. Otherwise, why engage in intimacy if your growth and love are served more by
living alone? Intimacy is about growing more than you could by yourself,
through the art of mutual gifting.

One of the largest gifts you can give your woman is your capacity to open her heart when it is closed. Sure, she can get herself out of her dark mood, but your masculine thunderbolt of love can brighten her darkness in a way she can't do for herself.

If you are like most men, however, you probably end up feeling burdened by your woman's mood. You feel your woman is a pain in the ass. You wish your woman would leave you alone and take care of herself. Eventually you feel worn down, or frustrated. You end up simply tolerating your woman's moods, while resentment builds inside of you. You wonder, what's her problem? Why can't she just be happy?

The feminine part of your woman is either opening in loving surrender (easy moments) or closing in what ends up being an emotional test of your capacity to open her (difficult moments). This cycle of the feminine is like all cycles in nature: it never ends. The sooner you learn to embrace and dance with these moods of closure, the sooner both of you will grow beyond the psychodrama and see the humor of the play.

Instead of tolerating your woman's moods of closure and complaint, open her moods with your skillful loving. It is your gift to give. Both of you will grow more by your giving than by your tolerating. A superior man sees his woman's moods not as a curse, but as a challenge and an amusement.

There are many ways to creatively deal with her moods and help her to open. Tickle her. Take off your clothes and dance the watusi. Sing opera for her. Make animal sounds. Shout at her louder than you ever have and then kiss her passionately. Press your belly into her until she melts. Lift her off the ground and spin her around. Occasionally, talking with her helps, but not as often as humor and physically expressed love.

If you have tried every creative, humorous, and powerful way of loving through her mood and she still refuses to let go of her closure, then simply relax. You have done everything you can. If you are not skillful enough to serve her, or she is not willing enough to receive your gifts, perhaps you are with the wrong woman.

Just remember that any woman you are with, if she has a feminine sexual essence, will cycle through moods of closure every day which seem to have no "reason" to them. You cannot avoid this by changing women or waiting for the moods to stop. You can only develop your skill in serving your woman into openness. It never ends though, even if you are passionate, fearless, loving, and humorous with her. The weather continually cycles through rainy and dry spells, night and day cycle in their turn, and your woman will continually cycle through openness and closure, even when her life and relationship with you seem great.

If you find yourself merely tolerating this feminine mood cycle because you have been frustrated by endless discussions that go nowhere, you can be sure that you and probably your woman are building up resentment toward each other. Don't tolerate her mood. And don't talk about it with her. Participate in it. Bloom her into fullness. Move her body with your body. Open her heart with your humor. Penetrate her closure with your fearless presence. Open her heart, again and again and again. She could do it by herself, but if she could grow more by herself than by receiving your gifts, perhaps she shouldn't be with you. ◆

19

Don't Analyze
Your Woman

*The feminine's moods and opinions are like
weather patterns. They are constantly changing,
severe and gentle, and they have no single source.
No analysis will work. There is no linear chain of
cause and effect that can lead to the kernel of the
"problem." There is no problem, only a storm, a
breeze, a sudden change in weather. And the bases
of these storms are the high and low pressure
systems of love. When a woman feels love flowing
deeply, her mood can instantly evaporate into joy,
regardless of the supposed reason for the mood.*

As a man, you probably want to find the cause for the problems in
your life. That way, you can eliminate the source of the problem.
By getting to its root, you can solve the problem, hopefully once and for
all. And so, when your woman seems to have an emotional problem, you
want to know why. You want to know what is upsetting her. You assume
there is a specific cause. You want to know what triggered her bad mood
so you can fix the situation.

Because you love her, you begin asking her questions to get to the root
of the problem. "What's wrong? Did I do something to upset you? What
are you crying about? Are you about to start your period? Did somebody
say something horrible to you?"

You are under the illusion that when you find out the cause of her affliction, then the cure will easily follow. But it doesn't work that way; your questioning is probably making her mood worse.

The amazing thing is this: 90% of a woman's emotional problems stem from feeling unloved. So don't stand back and analyze her, like a doctor diagnosing a patient, or like a therapist questioning a client. Give her your love—the same love that is motivating your questioning—immediately and unmistakably. Walk over to her, look deeply into her eyes, hold her and stroke her, tell her how much you love her, smile, hum her favorite song and dance with her, and chances are, her emotional problem will evaporate. She may still have some situation to deal with, and you may be able to help her with that, but the emotional aspect will be converted to love.

It is a very rare occasion when your analysis of her mood relieves her of it. Most often, your analysis and attempts to fix her will just piss her off more. Ask her if she would rather you gave her love or analyzed her when she is upset. It's so easy to give her love; it's what both of you really want anyway. But as a man you are more likely to try to fix her. That's exactly not what she wants, and exactly what will make the situation worse, most of the time.

The next time your woman is in a bad mood, try this: Assume she is not feeling loved. Simply assume it, even if it seems that it can't be that simple, that there must be some underlying reason for her upsetness, a reason that you could fix. Assume she is more like a flower that needs watering than an engine that needs a carburetor adjustment. Don't assume anything is wrong at all. Assume that she wants love from you, in a deep, strong, steady, and sensitive way.

Look into her eyes with love, touch her how she likes to be touched with love, and speak or sing to her with love. Discover what happens to her mood. Then, after her mood has been dissolved by your loving and she is happy and relaxed, you can talk about anything that still needs to be talked about.

If you ever find yourself asking your woman questions about her mood while she is still in it, you are already on the wrong road. First, give her love through your eyes, touch, movement, and tone of voice. Then and only then, after the connection of love has been made, find out what remains to be talked about. ◆

20 ◆

Don't Suggest That a Woman Fix Her Own Emotional Problem

Asking a woman to analyze or try to fix her own emotions is a negation of her feminine core, which is pure energy in motion, like the ocean. She can learn to surrender her mood to God, she can learn to open her heart in the midst of closure, she can learn to relax her edges and trust love, but she will never "fix" anything by analyzing her "problem."

As a man, you can learn a lot about yourself by clearly analyzing your problems. One of the best ways for you to grow is to use your discrimination, feeling what is causing unnecessary pain in your life, and then changing whatever you need to change. You may notice, for instance, that you are unhappy with your job. You think about it. You realize it is because your boss is taking advantage of you, and you haven't said anything to him. So, you determine that the best way to deal with the problem is to walk up to the boss and say something. You get up the guts, you walk up to the boss, you get it off your chest, and it's over. Problem fixed. Finished. You learned how important it is to talk to your boss, and you've cleared up all the old stuff that has been burdening you.

You probably apply the same system to your intimacy. You realize that you're not happy about something your wife is doing. Maybe you talk about it with your friends or think about it yourself. You realize that your wife isn't caring for you like she used to. So, you determine that you'll be happier if your wife cooks more and massages you more. You then think maybe your wife wants you to do something more for her. So you tell her what you want from her, and then you ask her, "What do you want from me?" You tell her to think about it and let you know.

This seems fair to a man, but it is not. It is a no-win situation for your woman. Why? Because what she really wants is a man who can figure it out for himself. She wants a man who loves her, and escorts her with his loving, without having to ask her what she wants all the time.

One of the deepest feminine desires in intimacy is precisely not to have to always figure it out for her man and guide him. She wants to be able to trust him in his direction. There are some times when she does want to figure it out for you, but far more often she feels your gift when you offer her a direction in your intimacy without her having to ask you for it or tell you what she wants.

Suppose it's your woman's birthday. If it were your birthday, you'd love it if your woman would do anything you wanted. So you think she'd like that, too. You say to her, "Happy Birthday! For your birthday, we can do anything you want. We can go anywhere and do anything. And I'll do anything for you. What do you want to do?"

This is exactly the opposite of most women's idea of an ideal birthday present. Most women would get far more excited if you were to say, "You've got 30 minutes to pack your bags. Don't ask me where we're going, but we'll be gone for the weekend. Everything is taken care of. Just pack your bags, and leave the rest to me. I'm going to give you the best birthday you've ever had."

One of the deepest feminine desires in intimacy (though not in business or simple friendship) is to be able to relax and surrender, knowing that her man is taking care of everything. Then, she can simply enjoy without having to plan it all herself and tell her man what to do. She can be pure energy, pure motion, pure love, without having to analyze all the options and decide which ones are best. She can enjoy her man taking responsibility for the direction, so she can be what the feminine is: pure energy.

Like the ocean, the native state of the feminine is to flow with great power and no single direction. The masculine builds canals, dams, and boats to unite with the power of the feminine ocean and go from point A to point B. But the feminine moves in many directions at once. The masculine chooses a single goal and moves in that direction. Like a ship cutting through a vast ocean, the masculine decides on a course and navigates the direction: the feminine energy itself is undirected but immense, like the wind and deep currents of the ocean, ever changing, beautiful, destructive, and the source of life.

This same principle applies to problems in intimacy. Any time you try to force your woman to be more like a ship than an ocean, you are negating her feminine energy. Any time you talk to her and expect her to analyze her mood and situation to the point of being able to fix it, you are talking "masculine" with her. She can do it, she might even be better at it than you, but it won't make her a happy woman.

A happy woman is a woman relaxed in her body and heart: powerful, unpredictable, deep, potentially wild and destructive, or calm and serene, but always full of life, surrendered to and moved by the great force of her oceanic heart. When you ask her to analyze her heart's emotions, it's like building walls around a part of the ocean and turning it into a swimming pool. It's safer and more predictable, but far less alive and enlivening. Most men have made their women into swimming pools by continually treating them like men, talking with them about their feelings as if they can be analyzed to the point of "fixing" them.

Don't waste your time doing this, but especially don't expect your woman to do it to herself. It would be like forcing you, a man, to read romance novels or watch love stories at the movies. Sure, you could do it. But it probably doesn't touch your core the way it touches hers. And, if she made you do it, over and over and over, you would begin to resent her. If she felt that the basic problem in your life is that you just don't watch enough soap opera on TV, you would think she was crazy.

Soap operas, romance novels, and love stories touch many women deeply because the feminine's priority is the flow of love in relationship. But the masculine priority is purpose and direction. By analyzing your purpose and re-aligning your direction, you can solve many of your emotional problems. But love is the feminine priority, not purpose and direction.

Women do not become free by analyzing themselves. They become free by surrendering into love. Not your love. Their love. They become free by surrendering to the immense flow of love that is native to their core and allowing their lives to be moved by this force in their heart. It may involve moments of analysis, but primarily it involves deep trust.

The best way you can serve your woman is by helping her to surrender, to trust the force of love, so that she can open her heart, be the love that she is, and give this love which naturally overflows from her happiness. THIS DOES NOT INVOLVE ANALYZING THE BLOCKS TO HER LOVING. Analyzing blocks is a man's way. Men love to analyze blocks, on the football field, the chess board, in the stock market, and even in their intimate life. But it's important that you, as a man, don't project your way of doing things onto your woman.

Let her be the ocean. Encourage her to be as free as the ocean, as deep as the ocean, as wild as the ocean, and as powerful as the ocean. Be so full in your loving, so strong and stable in your presence, that she can just let go and surrender the limits she has put on her feelings. Let the emotions of her heart flow unguarded. Let her love be expressed with no limits. Let her go mad with love.

Love has its own intelligence. Honor love's intelligence by realizing that analysis is not usually necessary to serve your woman's openness. Love your woman with your whole body, perhaps pressing her against the wall with your belly and chest, pressing your love into her, breathing with her so that she relaxes her tension and surrenders to the love in her heart, and let her relaxation and surrender liberate the wisdom inherent in her loving. You have much to gain from the depths of her feminine gifts. ◆

21

Stay With Her
Intensity—To a Point

*When a woman gets emotionally intense, a mediocre
man wants to calm her down and discuss it, or leave
and come back later when she is "sane." A superior
man penetrates her mood with imperturbable love
and unwavering consciousness. If she still refuses to
live more fully in love, after a time, he lets her go.*

I f you are like most men, you probably aren't too fond of feminine
bad moods and hysterical emotions. You may find yourself wondering,
why is she so complicated? What's her problem? You may find yourself
saying, "Just calm down and take it easy." The feminine bad mood is so
foreign and dark to you that you may actually find it somewhat repulsive.
And when your woman really goes wild, a part of you is afraid of the
damage she might do. Her emotions are so much more wild and less predictable than yours that you'd rather not be around them.

Basically, most men are afraid of, or disgusted by, feminine emotions.
That's why you try to fix them or escape from them. "I'll come back later
when you can act like a reasonable human being," you might say.

One of the deepest feminine pleasures is when a man stands full, present, and unreactive in the midst of his woman's emotional storms. When
he stays present with her, and loves her through the layers of wildness
and closure, then she feels his trustability, and she can relax.

The way you relate to your woman's chaos reflects the way you react to the chaos of the world. If you are the kind of man who needs everything placed neatly in its nice little box, then you will also try to box your woman's emotions. If you are the kind of man who would rather hire other people to take care of the chaos in your attic, or the chaos of your finances, you would probably also rather leave it to someone else to take care of the chaos of your woman.

You can, however, train yourself to master the world—financially, creatively, spiritually—by learning how to be free and loving in the chaos of your woman's emotions. And you do so by standing your ground and loving so strongly that only love prevails. You can't quit when you seem to fail, but rather, you must learn from your failures and return to love. Give your gift. Like wrestling a steer or surfing ocean waves, mastery involves blending with your woman's powerful energy and feeling the rise and fall of the moment, without lapsing in presence for a second.

You're going to get stamped on by the steer, you're going to get swamped by the ocean, and you're going to get hurt by your woman. This is how you learn. You get up, dust yourself off, swim to shore, and turn and face your woman again. The only options are fear or mastery. You can quit, you can choose small steer and tiny waves, you can wait for your woman to calm down, or you can even threaten her. Or, you can take the moment as a challenge to your ability to conquer the world, and your woman, with love.

Keep your breath full. Keep your body strong. Keep your attention present. No matter what your woman says or does, give her love. Press your belly into her. Smile. Scream and then lick her face. Do whatever it takes to crack the shell of her closure, get your love inside that crack, and touch her heart. Learn to enjoy her anger, her tears, her silent hardness. The world will give you the same at times.

The game of life is to find each situation workable, to transform each occasion through the magnification of love, to give your fullest gift in every moment, and to have no attachments to the outcome, knowing it's all going to rise and fall and rise again.

You have mastered women and the world when no desire either to avoid or attain sways your loving or limits your freedom. ◆

22

Don't Force the Feminine
to Make Decisions

*A man abandons responsibility by expecting that
his woman will always make her own decisions
and then be accountable for the results. This
expectation is a withholding of his masculine gift.
It puts a woman in the position of magnifying her
own masculine. It is good for some women to learn
to animate their masculine capacity to make a
decision and stick with it. But if a man abnegates
his responsibility to provide his woman with the gift
of masculine clarity and decisiveness, then she will
become chronically sharp, angular, and distrustful
of his love. She will cease surrendering in love
with him, cease trusting his masculine capacity,
and, instead, become her own man.*

Your woman asks you for input, and you say, "Whatever you want to do is fine with me." This is the statement of a friend, not a lover. As friends, you want to treat each other fairly and give each other space and independence. As lovers, you and your woman are more than just friends. You are playing the full dynamic of masculine and feminine polarity. Wouldn't you like your woman to be a goddess and offer you her feminine gifts? To evoke them, you must offer her your masculine gifts.

One of your most valuable gifts is the ability to see all the options and make a decision based on this view of all the potential outcomes.

Feminine decisions are based on what feels right, and often this is the best way to make a decision. However, the point in intimacy is not simply to make the best decision, but to make the best decision while maintaining the force of masculine/feminine polarity that attracted you together to begin with. If that polarity begins to diminish, conflicts will begin to increase. When that polarity disappears, attraction disappears, and the life of the intimacy disappears with it.

You need to play the masculine pole if you want your woman to play the feminine. Offering your perspective on decisions is one way to give your masculine gift. Eve on the most trivial decisions, never say, "Do whatever you want." If she asks you which shoes you think look better on her, make a decision, and tell her. Don't just say, "They're both nice." Say something like, "I'd like the red shoes, but what's the most important to me is that you're happy." She is of course free to wear whatever she wants, but she is also the recipient of your masculine gift of decisiveness.

Perhaps your woman is trying to make a career decision, something that will affect her for many years. She might feel into it, and do what feels best to her, which would be a feminine style of making a decision. Or, she might be trying to make a decision based on the different possible outcomes of her choices, which would be a masculine style. Because you have a masculine sexual essence, you will naturally be able to contribute to her masculine decision process. And, more importantly for the intimacy, if you don't contribute to her masculine decision making process, the two of you will become depolarized by each other's energy. She'll be in the masculine, you'll be neutral, and there will be nobody in the feminine pole This is fine for short periods of time, but if it becomes chronic, then the two of you will begin to feel like friends rather than lovers. The attractive juiciness of polarity will be replaced by two buddies discussing options.

If you refuse to offer your masculine gift by saying things like, "I don't really care. It's up to you," then she will have to learn to depend on her own masculine capacity. Another way to say this is that she will begin to trust her own masculine more than yours. Then, you will find that she trusts you less and less across the board. She will refuse to surrender to you even sexually, because she hasn't been able to relax and trust you all day; you haven't offered her your masculine clarity and perspective, so she has to be her own man and give it to herself.

As a practice, always help your woman make decisions by giving her your perspective and telling her your choices, while letting her know that you love her regardless of the decision she makes. Often her feminine feelings will be a much better basis for a decision than your masculine analysis. So, encourage her to feel into the situation and trust her feelings. But, for the sake of polarity and happiness in intimacy, always tell her what you would do and why, even if you think she should make her own decision. ◆

PART

THREE

*Working With
Polarity and Energy*

23

Your Attraction to the Feminine Is Inevitable

Masculine men are attracted to forms of feminine energy: radiant women, beer, music, nature, etc. If a man tries to hide his attraction, it reveals some degree of shame with respect to his own sexual core.

▼

I f you are like most men, you probably hide the amount of sexual attraction you feel toward women every day. At work, on the street, and in the grocery store, you see women that turn you on. Sometimes you might want to have sex with them. But many times the feeling is more of a wave of refreshment washing through you. Seeing an especially radiant woman can fill your whole day with delight. A woman's exquisite scent can transport you to an enchanted paradise. A woman's smile can melt the moment into sheer beatitude.

There are two ways to deal with your daily "ahhh" of attraction to the feminine: wisely and foolishly. To respond wisely, you must understand why you are attracted to whom. Your sexual essence is always attracted to its energetic reciprocal. Masculine men are attracted to feminine women. Feminine men are attracted to masculine women. Balanced men are attracted to balanced women.

About 80% of all men have a more masculine sexual essence. These men, of which you are probably one, are attracted to all things feminine. Not just feminine women, but anything with feminine energy, anything which is radiant, alive, enlivening, relaxing, and moving. Feminine energy gets you out of your head and into your body. Music, beer, nature, women, they are all forms of feminine energy.

It is not just a visually gorgeous woman who attracts you. If a woman is free and radiant in her feminine energy, you are probably attracted; sometimes more attracted, sometimes less attracted, but always attracted, at least enough to steal a glance at her form. This attraction is not only natural, but healthy. It is a sign of polarity, the same kind of natural flow of polarization by which electricity flows between the positive and negative poles of a battery. It's nothing to be ashamed of. It's why there *are* men and women. The nature of nature is polarity, from the magnetism that flows between the North and South Poles of the Earth, to the attraction that flows between your masculine core and the feminine radiance of a woman.

If you feel uncomfortable with your attraction to women, you are probably uncomfortable with your own masculine essence. If you feel it is demeaning for a woman to be the "object" of your polar attraction, then you have probably disowned your masculine core. You have energetically emasculated yourself by condemning and suppressing your native desires. You are negating your sexual essence, rather than being at home with it.

Any negative attitude you have about your attraction to women is a sign of fear; somewhere along the line you learned that such attraction was "bad" or "evil." Your attraction to women, all kinds of women, is natural, normal, and beautiful. In fact, it is an aspect of the same desire that will ultimately lead you toward spiritual freedom.

Your desire for a woman is an aspect of your desire for pleasurable oneness. Your confession of desire is a confession of your desire to embrace life. To embrace life, to relax into oneness so that all opposites, including masculine and feminine, find their unity in love, is to be spiritually free. Eventually you will recognize that all desire is an aspect of your native impulse to give love. From beginning to end, your attraction to women can be seen as the essential gesture of your heart, your desire for love and unity.

If you are a man with a masculine sexual essence, you will always feel sexual polarity with anyone who animates feminine energy. You may feel this attraction many times a day, with many women. Enjoy it. Women are a blessing! The feminine, even in the non-human forms of a lush tropical island, a cold beer, or your favorite tune, could make the difference between dreariness and ahhh-ing in ecstasy. Our acceptance of sexual attraction, even with music and places, is at the root of our capacity to experience bodily pleasure.

Sexual attraction, however, is very different from having sex. There is a big difference between choosing to be intimate with a woman and simply being attracted to her energy and radiance. Intimacy is a choice between people who want to commit to loving and serving one another. Whereas the zing of attraction is a choiceless natural flow of energy between your masculine core and feminine energy, wherever it is found. When a woman is relaxed in her feminine radiance, she is like beautiful music or a warm ocean breeze. You don't need to have sex with her to savor inexpressible joy.

If you are like most men, a radiant woman can inspire you for hours or days. Remember, the desire she arouses in you is a blessing in itself. Acting on that desire and pursuing her is another matter entirely, dependent on whether such an action would truly serve both of you or not. But the mere inspiration felt while beholding a radiant woman is one of nature's gifts to you: the gift of feminine blessing.

The next time you come upon a woman who sends a thrill through your body, relax into the thrill. Let her waves of feminine energy move through your body like a deep massage. Breathe fully, without resisting the joy her sighting affords you. Breathe the joy all through your body, down to your toes. Don't stare at her, don't even interact with her. But when you see her, and you experience your attraction, fully allow the energy of attraction to move freely through your body. Learn to magnify and sustain your desire, so your whole body and breath open and deepen by its force. As you behold her, receive her vision as a blessing. ◆

24

Choose a Woman Who Is Your Complementary Opposite

If a man is very masculine by nature, then he will be attracted to a very feminine woman, who will complement his energy. The more neutral or balanced he is, the more balanced he will prefer his woman. And, if a man is more feminine by nature, his energy will be complemented by the strong direction and purposiveness of a more masculine woman. By understanding their own needs, men can learn to accept the "whole package" of a woman. For instance, a more masculine man can expect that any woman who really turns him on and enlivens him will also be relatively wild, undisciplined, "bonkers," chaotic, prone to changing her mind and "lying." Still, from an energetic perspective, this kind of woman will be much more healing and inspiring to him than a more balanced or neutral woman who is steady, reasonable, "trustworthy," and able to say what she means in a way he can understand.

You have probably met a woman who seemed fantastic, only to discover she has some emotional weirdness that you don't really want to deal with. She seemed incredibly sexy, but also a bit "bonkers" or crazy, saying one thing one moment and another the next. You have probably also met some very reasonable and trustworthy women who don't seem to constantly change their mind and, in fact, with whom you could have good conversations that don't end up frustrating you. Although you may love these women and enjoy spending time with them, they don't arouse your passion as much as the women whose words you wouldn't trust to remain true for an afternoon, but who move their body in a way that drives you wild.

"Why can't a woman be more like a man?" many men have wondered. But, of course, it is precisely those ways in which a woman is least like a man that most attract you sexually, if you have a masculine sexual essence. A woman's feminine shine, the energy that moves her body, her utterly refreshing spontaneity and mystery, not to mention her delightful smile, are what attract you. And the more feminine a woman is at her core, the less she is likely to evidence strong masculine traits, such as speaking clearly and unequivocally about thoughts and desires, rather than primarily expressing her feelings of the moment.

A woman with a more feminine sexual essence will say she loves you one moment, and then, when you have done something you are not even aware of, she will say she hates you. This is the beauty of the feminine; to her, the masculine grid of words and events is less relevant than the fluidity of relationship and feeling. Thank God for such women, who make no apologies for their oceanic depth and riptides of emotion.

You are always attracted to your sexual reciprocal. So, if you have a more feminine sexual essence, you will be attracted to a more masculine woman. You have probably seen men and women in couples like this. The man is more radiant and lively than the woman. The woman is more committed to her direction in life than the man. The relationship is more important to the man, whereas the woman likes to be left alone much of the time. These are signs of a relationship where the man has a more feminine essence and the woman's essence is more masculine.

Other men, with more neutral sexual essences, prefer women who are also more neutral, neither particularly masculine nor feminine. This kind of couple can talk about anything, and they like talking about everything. They share hobbies, friends, even career goals. Though equally loving, this kind of couple is usually less sexually passionate than highly polarized couples. It would be unusual to hear about this kind of neutral or balanced couple yelling at each other, throwing pillows, wrestling each other down to the floor, and passionately making love right there and then.

Through lack of understanding, you might have depolarized yourself and your partner into a relationship that seems neutral, but actually isn't. Only about 10% of couples are actually the neutral or balanced type in their true essence. Another 10% of couples are made up of a feminine man and masculine woman. But if you are like 80% of couples, you have a masculine sexual essence and your woman has a feminine one. That is, her feminine way frustrates you, drives you crazy, inspires you, or turns you on, more often than she is simply your sexually neutral buddy.

The false neutralization, or depolarization, of relationships is one of the main reasons that couples break up. The rejuvenative charge of sexual loving becomes weak, while all the things that irritate you and your partner remain just as strong as ever. The secret is not to try to change your woman's irritating feminine ways, but to help cultivate the depth and rejuvenative power of her feminine blessings.

If you are like most men, you have probably minimized your appreciation of the full spectrum of your woman's feminine energy by numbing yourself to the aspects that most irritate you. For instance, she doesn't drive you crazy any more because you've learned not to take her too seriously. Perhaps you have learned to seem attentive while not really listening to her endless chat. Or, maybe you have learned to give her a daily dose of affection as a way to quell her ongoing need for more intimate time than you really want to spend with her.

This is the wrong approach. The feminine is an infinite source of love, inspiration, and power, both physically and spiritually. Feminine women are connected with the elements of nature in ways that more masculine people, such as yourself, usually aren't. Feminine women may seem wild, untrustable, or even irresponsible from a man's perspective, but such women are simply free of the masculine need to live in a world governed by reason and control.

Feminine women are free to feel flows of natural livingness that you are unable to feel. They are free to be moved by currents of energy of which most men are unaware. They are free to allow their bodies to be transparent to the flow of their hearts, uncontrolled and undirected by goals and structure. The feminine body is free to be moved by love, and by life itself. And this is highly valued by most men; to behold a woman free in her expression of bodily ecstasy is one of the most awesome visions most men have had.

Men will even pay to watch a woman's body express ecstasy, even if she is only faking it, like in a porn movie. In our secular culture, most men are only familiar with sexual ecstasy, and so it is this form of free bodily expression that men pay to see, in movies, on the stage, and in private rooms around the world. However, in cultures that admit a greater degree of spiritual revelation, women's bodies are viewed with the same masculine awe, but for a different kind of expression: not merely for their capacity to express sexual ecstasy in a way that is foreign, and unbelievably attractive, but also for their capacity to express spiritual ecstasy.

Temple dancers in India, for instance, are traditionally feminine women trained from an early age to combine skill and heartfelt devotion in a style of dance which frees their bodies to be moved by divine force, bringing tears to many men's eyes and openness to their hearts. A woman who is at home with her feminine essence is at home with energy, be it sexual or spiritual. For such a woman, there is no disconnection between sex and spirit. Her sexual surrender, if she is with a worthy man, is the same as her devotional or spiritual surrender. She opens from head to toe, receiving divine love-force deep throughout her body, so that she is rippled, arched, and undulated by its boundless flow.

More masculine or neutral women are less likely to allow such freedom of bodily expression. Yet it is a woman's expression of this kind of ecstasy that invites a masculine man to leave his heady world of thoughts and goals and celebrate the moment, in the flesh, through the heart. Whether in a strip joint or a sacred temple, men have been attracted for thousands of years to witness the feminine embodiment of ecstasy. Women are literally worshipped in such occasions. Men shout their praises to the goddess dancing before them in ways they would never do in public. The fullest of such occasions is completely sexual and completely spiritual at the same time. Men leave such an event transformed and inspired by the blessing power of free feminine embodiment. This is one of the unique gifts of the feminine form, of woman.

This is what you get in a woman with a feminine sexual essence: A woman who is all over the place emotionally. A woman whom you can depend on to change her mind. A woman who is much more sensitive than you are to the flow of subtle energies in your relationship. A woman who brings you delight and awe in the ecstasy, both sexual and spiritual, that her body expresses so freely and beautifully.

It is all one package. You can't have a woman who is always logically consistent, reasonable, and on time, and who also fills your heart and flesh with energy, instantly and throughout the day, with her bodily expressed love and ecstasy. She can animate reasonable masculine energy when she wants, but if she has a feminine core, much of the time she will want to dance, in wrathful anger or enchanting joy, beyond the need for reason.

So, choose a woman who is your complementary opposite, which for most men means a more feminine woman. It is only a feminine woman who can give the gifts that you, as a masculine man, need. Along with these gifts, however, come the relative chaos and emotional weather storms that most men dread. Realize these are aspects of the same energy that turns you on. In fact, you can learn to be turned on by her dance of anger as much as by her slinky purr. This capacity is one of your gifts to her. You can learn to stand free and strong no matter what emotion she displays. You won't leave, turn away, or dissociate in disgust. You can meet her enormous energy and stand full, loving her through the storm, embracing her complete feminine power, dark and light.

You will only be happy in intimacy if you choose a woman who is your sexual reciprocal as a partner. And you will only be able to survive such an intimacy if her dark and light sides are equally embraceable to you. It takes time to develop such skill and strength, but in doing so you learn to provide your woman, as well as the world, with a man whose gifts are uncompromised by fear of feminine power and chaos. ◆

25

Know What Is
Important in Your Woman

*The feminine is the force of life. The more masculine a
man is, the more his woman's feminine energy
(as opposed to other qualities) will be important to him.*

▼

I f you are looking for a woman business partner, you probably want
certain qualities in her, such as financial acumen, dependability, and
the capacity to persist in the face of difficulties in order to achieve a
goal. If you are looking for a woman friend, you probably want honesty,
compassion, humor, and respect. If you are looking for a consort, you
probably want a woman who freely embodies and expresses feminine
energy and love.

The more you seek a woman who gives you everything, the less you
get of anything. Business skills are for the most part masculine skills (in
both men and women). Friendship, in itself, is a neutral, nonsexual matter. And sexual passion requires a clear polarity between your masculine
core and your woman's feminine energy. When you don't prioritize the
purpose of your relationship, these different energies often cancel each
other out, and you are left with a sexually neutralized alliance.

You can share many aspects of intimacy—business, friendship, parenting, and sexual passion—only if you choose a single priority to the
relationship and allow all the other activities to align themselves around
your main purpose for being together. If you aren't clear about what's important, though, each aspect will conflict with the others. She will want

affection when you want to get business done. She will want to talk about her day when you want to have sex. You will both end up compromising your true desires, and your relationship will be reduced to a functional but mediocre partnership.

Over time, sexual polarity and attraction will diminish. You will begin eyeing other women as sources of rejuvenative feminine delight, the same delight you have smeared out in your intimacy by obliging your woman to be everything for you all blurred together: your business partner one moment, your friend another moment, a mother this moment, and your lover the next. Eventually, the deep gifts that brought you together to begin with become lost in the ambiguity of your relationship.

In other times and cultures, you might have had multiple intimate partners, each fulfilling a different purpose, each partner contributing different skills, functions, and sexual energies to the whole. In our modern world, however, polygamy is not much of an option. For social and psychological reasons, most men and women of today want to limit their intimate scope to one committed partner at a time—although, if you are like most men, you've certainly entertained the notion of multiple wives, or at least a mistress or two, each fulfilling a different purpose.

Because you expect your intimate relationship to serve so many purposes, it begins to veer toward the utilitarian. By constantly talking about finances, work, household, and children, you turn your woman into a neutral companion. You become so familiar with each other that the mystery of sexual enchantment becomes standardized into the ritual mechanics of kiss, stroke, lick, pump, spurt, and snore. You begin to long for the depth of desire you once felt with your woman. Domesticity replaces mystery, and talk replaces tumble.

Yet, if you have a strong masculine sexual essence, you will need frequent refreshment by the power of strong feminine energy or else you will begin to feel weary and burdened by life. You may seek this rejuvenative feminine energy in a few beers, a few rounds of golf, or a few girlie magazines. Or perhaps you favor long massages and walks on the beach. Although these and many other means can temporarily relax you and put a smile on your face, few of them can arouse you as deeply in heart and body as the uncompromised force of feminine sexuality offered by your radiant woman in love.

You are the only one who can decide what is important to you in your relationship. You are the only one who can clarify for yourself what the purpose of your intimacy is. If you decide, however, that the purpose of your intimacy is the passionate transmission of love, the rejuvenative healing of sexual energy, and the cultivation of heart through your mutual commitment to spiritual awakening, then be careful. Don't force your woman to be your on-call accountant. Don't expect her to always help you with your financial problems, like a career consultant. Don't emphasize the daily chores while disregarding the bodily transmission of love for days and days. Don't squash the fullness of her feminine energy into merely functional roles. Your woman has the capacity to awaken your heart and fill your body with life. You, however, must give her the opportunity—as well as the fullness of your masculine transmission of love.

If you want your woman to be your spiritual and sexual consort, not just your housemate, you must skillfully maintain your household and livelihoods so that the potency of your union is not diminished. She can be the mother of your children as well as your business partner, as long as these functions do not cut into the primacy of your purpose: to serve one another's enlightenment through your unwavering commitment to love, and to enliven one another's core by the bodily transmission of love via sexual polarity.

When these two aspects of your loving—spiritual awakening and sexual transmission—become diminished by your daily duties, you will both begin to seek elsewhere for daily refreshment and fulfillment. You will seek feminine energy in the form of a six-pack or a mistress. Your woman will seek masculine direction in the form of a social cause or a masculine-style career. Your relationship will become relegated to a well-meaning partnership of domestic duty. This may be exactly what you want. Or it may not be. In any case, you must know what is important for you, what is the purpose of your intimacy, and align all other activities around this central priority, if you want your intimacy to maintain and increase its potency for both of you. ◆

26

You Will Often Want
More Than One Woman

*Any man with a masculine sexual essence will
desire sexual variety. Even if he loves his intimate
partner and is completely committed to her, he will
naturally want sexual occasions with other women
besides his chosen intimate partner. How a man
deals with his desire for other women is up to him.
He should know, however, that there is no way to
avoid such desires. He should also know that acting
on such desires, though temporarily enlivening and
exhilarating, often ends up complicating his life
far more than the occasion itself is worth.*

▼

Even if you are totally committed to your intimate partner in love,
you probably think about having sex with other women. Even if
you are totally fulfilled by the sex you share with your woman, you probably still desire sex with other women. Your desire for other women is
not a reflection of any lack in your intimacy, it is a reflection of your nature as a masculine sexual being.

But this desire is not an excuse for promiscuity, any more than your
enjoyment of TV is an excuse for becoming an obese couch potato. Desire springs from many sources, such as your addictions, your biological
heritage, your childhood conditioning, and your open heart. To live a life
of impeccable integrity, you must discriminate the source of your desire,

so you know when to discipline your behavior for everyone's benefit, including yours.

The fact is you probably want to have sex with other women besides your intimate partner; how you respond to this fact is a reflection of your purpose in life. If your purpose is to enjoy physical pleasure no matter the consequences, then you should screw as many women as you want. If your purpose is to be a nice boy and please "mommy," then you should do what makes your woman happy. If your purpose is to liberate yourself and others into love and freedom, then you should do whatever magnifies the love and freedom in your life and in the lives of those whom your actions affect.

It's your call. Just remember that self-discipline is not self-suppression. Suppression is when you resist and fight against your desires, keeping them as buried and unexpressed as possible. Self-discipline is when your highest desires rule your lesser desires, not through resistance, but through loving action grounded in understanding and compassion.

How many women you have sex with is your business. Before you consider more than one, however, it is best to prove your capacity with one. If you can't handle one—if deep communion, rejuvenating passion, and spiritual happiness are not the main features of your present intimacy—then you have not passed the test, and it is best to discipline your desire for other partners, since nobody is likely to be served. ◆

27
Young Women Offer
You a Special Energy

In general, youth in a woman bespeaks radiant,
unobstructed, and refreshing feminine energy. A young
woman tends to be less compromised by masculine
layers of functional protection built up over years of
need. Traditionally, young women were understood
to offer a man a particularly rejuvenative quality of
energy. Older women may maintain, or even increase,
the freshness and radiance of their energy, but it is rare.

Imagine you are driving your eighteen year old babysitter home one evening. She is so fresh, so innocent, so alive. You can feel that she is totally open to you. You consider all the consequences. You look at her radiant skin, her clear eyes, her incredible smile. The way she moves, talks, and laughs makes you happy and fills you with energy. You arrive at her home. She says goodnight, leaves the car, and enters her house. You sit in the car for a moment, breathing slowly and deeply, smiling.

There is something unique about being with a young woman, and all men with masculine sexual essences feel it. You feel rejuvenated by her. Just sitting next to a young woman can make you happy and fill you with life force. You might have nothing in common. But that doesn't matter. It is her energy that delights and inspires you.

Uncompromised, youthful, feminine energy turns you on and opens your heart. You actually feel happier around young women. You feel more energetic, alive, and loving. As women get older, they typically take on more and more masculine tasks and responsibilities in our culture, so their radiance begins to decrease. In other cultures, this is less true. Women maintain and even deepen their radiance. But even in these cultures with more wisdom, it is understood that young women provide a special energy that is fresh, uncompromised, and enlivening.

Our culture reduces this youthful energy to a sexual thing, whereas it is actually a whole body transmission of energy, affecting the heart as much as or more than the genitals. In other cultures, young women were honored for their gifts of spiritual rejuvenation, tending to holy sites and performing sacred arts, not just ogled for sexual titillation. As a man, it is your responsibility to honor the heart-rejuvenative gift of a young woman, without violating this honor by imposing your sexual desire on her.

If sexual desire arises, fine. Circulate it through your body. Learn to conduct the magnification of desire without needing to throw it off in a spasm of release. A major part of mastering sexuality is learning to sustain greater and greater degrees of pleasure and desire in the body, without needing to rid yourself of the force because you can't handle it.

When you find yourself really enlivened by a young woman, breathe in her fragrance. Breathe in her energy. Relax your body and allow your heart to open in her presence. Take in her beauty through every pore in your body. Allow love to radiate from your heart toward her. Maintain a respectful formality so that she is free and empowered to give her gift, without being complicated by your personal agenda. Use the energy she has given you in your own service to others, passing the gifts of heightened aliveness and passionate heart into all of your relationships, so that all beings may benefit by the delight you have received from this woman, who, for now, manifests the youthful gifts of uncompromised radiance and life force ◆

28

Each Woman Has a "Temperature" That Can Heal or Irritate You

Some women are hotter, some are cooler. In general, blonde, light-skinned, Japanese, and Chinese women are cooler. Dark skinned, brunette, red-headed, Korean, and Polynesian women are hotter. Even though a man might choose to remain in a committed intimacy with one woman, his needs for different temperatures of feminine energy may change over time. A hot woman who aroused his passion several years ago may irritate him now. A cooler woman who soothed his heart several years ago may seem tiresome to him now. By understanding how different temperatures of feminine energy may affect him, a man could make more skillful life choices without confusion.

You probably have certain "tastes" in women. You might prefer blondes. Or Asian women. Or perhaps you have a special preference for redheads. Your tastes come from many sources: your early childhood experience, cultural influence, and perhaps even your genetics. But one aspect of "taste" has to do with how a woman affects you with her energetics.

Some women are cooling. Being in their company feels like a cool drink of ice tea on a hot sunny day. You might have referred to a woman, for instance, who is an "icy blonde" or who has "cool blue eyes."

Other women are hot. They are fiery, tempestuous, and quick of temper. You might have spoken of a "fiery red-head" or a "hot-blooded Latina."

Of course, not all red-heads or Latinas are hot, nor are all blondes cool. Nevertheless, there is something true enough to be said about a woman's "temperature." Most men have a good intuitive sense of the difference between a woman who is cool and soothing and a woman who is hot and exciting, regardless of how they describe it. And this difference has a lot to do with why men have different tastes for women, and why your taste could change over time.

More than simple psychological preference determines your taste. Energy plays a major role. Sometimes you can be with a beautiful woman who just doesn't do it for you. You can see she is beautiful, you can understand why your friends find her attractive, but she just doesn't suit your taste. Different women offer different kinds of feminine energy. And one of the simplest forms of this difference is the difference between hot and cool feminine energy.

To help understand this, you could look at your relationship with food. Some men thrive on hot Mexican peppers or spicy Szechwan food, while other men are healed by soothing and cooling food, like salads, sweets, or milk. And any man's needs for different kinds of food may change over time. The same is true of his needs for feminine energy.

If you are a particularly easygoing man, perhaps a man who has difficulty getting motivated, then a hot woman is probably better for you. Her fiery nature can heat up your system and get you moving. On the other hand, if you tend to be quick tempered and hot yourself, you might find that a more cooling woman heals you and brings a balance to your body and psyche.

Depending on your health, your lifestyle, your work demands, and your emotional state, you may need different types of energy at different times. The important thing is to know there is a difference, so that you can be conscious of the choice you are making and how it might affect you.

You may begin to doubt your current intimate relationship if you don't understand how your needs for feminine energy change. When your life seems dreary and boring, a more spicy and hot woman will probably appeal to you. She will provide you with the fire you are missing. However, when your life is extremely challenging and you feel burnt out, a hot woman might be too much. You may be more attracted to the soothing gaze and touch of a cool woman.

Imagine you are married to a hot woman. For years you have enjoyed her passion, been amused by her anger, and been delighted by how quickly she responds sexually. Then, your career takes a turn. You begin working with people all day, under a tight deadline. You are dealing with people's emotions and resistance 50 hours a week. You notice that you are sweating most of the day. You are under the gun. Your life has become quite hot, as if you are spending the day in a pressure cooker.

You go home to your hot wife. She is rubbing herself all over you, eager to get it on. You feel like relaxing. You tell her you need a few minutes to take it easy, so she changes into her workout clothes and goes to the spa to flex and pump her supple body. Meanwhile, her best friend comes to visit. You open the door and invite her in the house. She moves so much more slowly than your wife. Her presence seems soothing and relaxing to you, even though she's not the kind of woman you are usually attracted to.

The quality of this woman's voice seems so refreshing. She sees you are tired and, because she's known you for years, she asks if she can rub your shoulders. She puts her hands on your shoulders, and, before she even begins to gently massage you, you feel waves of cool, rejuvenating energy pour into your body. You sigh with relief. After a brief massage she says good-bye. She'll come back and visit your wife another day.

Your wife comes back home, full of energy, and she begins bouncing around the house taking care of things. She yells at you for not telling her friend to stay and wait. Then, seeing your fatigue, she apologizes and begins kissing you passionately. Her hands quickly go to your crotch, but you're still thinking about her friend, remembering how refreshing her energy was, wondering what the heck you're going to do about it.

What you should do about it is this: understand what is happening. You used to really enjoy your wife's spicy temperament, but now that you are boiling all day at work, you need to be balanced by a cooler energy. This doesn't mean you need to end your marriage. It doesn't necessarily mean you need to have sex with her cool friend. What is means is that you need to find a way to balance your life.

You can change your diet to a more cooling diet. You can keep your body cooler, wearing caps on sunny days, and wearing lighter, more breathable clothing. You can take soothing walks around lakes or along rivers, and let the water absorb the heat of your day. Or, you can receive cooling energy directly from a woman, even non-sexually.

You could get a professional massage, for instance, from a woman with cooling energy. Sometimes all you need to do is spend a little time in the same room with a cool woman. In any case, it's important to realize that your needs for different kinds of energy will change throughout your life. It's something you will need to learn how to deal with. It's important that, in the meantime, you don't mistake a changing energy need for a reason to end your marriage. It's also important to know that you can receive energy from different women in entirely non-sexual ways, if you so choose.

In the end, you must make your own choice. When one man's energy needs change and he finds himself getting the energy he needs from the woman in the office next door—the kind of energy that he isn't getting from his wife—then he might end up having an affair, or getting divorced. Another man might communicate his changing energy needs to his wife, then find that she is more than able to creatively provide him with the flavor of feminine energy that most heals and rejuvenates him.

Don't confuse your energy needs with a commitment in love, though. Energy needs are relatively easy to balance. You can probably get the energy you need from a masseuse or a change in diet. If you react drastically, and decide to leave your wife for a woman whose energy enlivens you more, you may be surprised when, in a few months, your energy needs change again, and you realize you have made a very superficial choice.

You must decide for yourself how to deal with your need for the particular feminine energy that fills your body with life, heals your rough edges, and soothes your warrior spirit. But energetic rejuvenation won't make any fundamental difference unless, at your core, your heart is growing more free, open and loving. A cool glass of fruit juice, a vacation in Hawaii, or a red-head may temporarily balance your physiology, but only persistent commitment to the practice of love can take you through your fears, through your sense of separateness, and bring you to the absolute ease of being that is your deepest truth. Remember your priority, and decide what you need to do. ◆

PART

FOUR

*What Women
Really Want*

29

Choose a Woman Who Chooses You

If a man wants a woman who doesn't want him, he cannot win. His neediness will undermine any possible relationship, and his woman will never be able to trust him. A man must determine whether a woman really wants him but is playing hard to get, or whether she really doesn't want him. If she doesn't want him, he should immediately cease pursuing her and deal with his pain by himself.

▼

If you ever find yourself in a situation where you want to be with a woman but she doesn't want to be with you, you must speak with your friends. Ask them to be honest with you. Ask them if they think this woman really does want to be with you, or if she really doesn't.

If your friends honestly tell you that this woman doesn't want to be with you, it is over. You cannot enjoy a good relationship with her, even if she changes her mind. Once she feels your neediness, once she feels that you need her more than she needs you, she will never trust your masculine core.

The priority of the masculine core is mission, purpose, or direction in life. The priority of the feminine core is the flow of love in intimacy. If a woman feels your feminine is stronger than hers—if she feels that the intimacy is more important to you than to he—then she will naturally animate her masculine. She will want space, she will want freedom to pursue her own direction, and she will be repulsed by your clinginess.

You are only punishing yourself when you want to be in a relationship with a woman more than she wants to be a in a relationship with you. Of course, you must discriminate between whether she is playing "hard to get" or whether she is genuinely less interested in the relationship than you. This is why you should ask your friends, and even her friends. If it turns out that she really doesn't want to be with you as much as you want to be with her, then it is time to realize the relationship won't work. In such a case, the poles have become reversed, with your feminine desire for love meeting her masculine desire for freedom. This is not viable grounds for intimacy between a man with a masculine essence and a woman with a feminine essence. It is better to move on and work with your hurt than it is to continue demonstrating that your feminine desire is stronger than hers. ◆

30

What She Wants
Is Not What She Says

Sometimes a woman will make a request of her man in plain English, not to get him to do something, but to see if he is so weak that he will do it. In other words, she is testing his capacity to do what is right, not what she is asking for. In such cases, if the man does what his woman asks, she will be disappointed and angry. The man will have no idea why she is so angry or what could possibly please her. He must remember that her trust is engendered not by him fulfilling her requests, but by him magnifying love, consciousness, and success in their lives, in spite of her requests.

This is a true story. A somewhat quiet and sensitive man was learning sexual yoga. In this yoga it is important to learn to bypass ejaculation, circulating the stimulated energy through the body and heart in a kind of whole body orgasm, rather than losing energy in a spasm of ejaculative release. He was also learning to express his animal-like passion instead of always remaining calm and passive during sex.

One day, this man and his wife were driving in their car. Passing a park, they spontaneously decided to stop the car, run into the woods, and make wild love on the grass beneath the trees. Neither of them had even made love outdoors before. Here they were, clawing at each other, growling, shrieking, passionately aggressive with one another. It was a real breakthrough for them.

Suddenly, the man realized he would ejaculate unless they slowed down for a few seconds. "Stop moving for a bit," he told his wife. "If we keep going like this, I'm going to come."

But the woman kept moving, even more vigorously. "I want you to come inside of me," she begged. "I want you to fill me with your seed."

The man had a split second to decide which way he was going to go, and he decided to let go and give his woman her wish. He ejaculated inside of her, and relaxed.

But when he looked at his wife's face, she was clearly upset. "What's wrong?" he asked her.

"You came," she answered.

"But you said you wanted me to fill you with my seed, didn't you?"

"Yes, but I said that in order to feel that you were strong enough not to!"

The man felt depleted and empty. He felt he had failed in his practice of sexual yoga. He knew that ejaculating had not been the right thing to do in the moment, but he had succumbed to his wife's wish. Now, she was disappointed. When she said to fill her with his seed, she really wanted to feel that he was strong enough to maintain what he knew was right, and not ejaculate. That would have been much more erotic to her, more polarizing, and more trust-producing than his obedience to her request to ejaculate.

Your woman probably tests you in this way all the time. Her ultimate desire is to feel your full consciousness, your trustable integrity, your unshakable love, and your confidence in your mission. Yet she will rarely ask you directly for these things. She would rather try to distract you from your truth, and then feel that she cannot—that you hold fast to your truth while you continue to love her.

If you are a weak man, this feminine trait of wanting one thing and asking for another will piss you off. You will wonder, "Why don't you just tell me what you really want, instead of saying one thing and meaning another, expecting me to figure it out?" This is the view of a man who does not understand that women are an incarnation of the divine feminine. And the divine feminine settles for nothing less than the divine masculine.

The divine masculine is consciousness. A superior man practices maintaining full consciousness in all situations. If ejaculation results in a decrease of your fullness, a diminution of your presence, a collapse of your consciousness, then you should not ejaculate. Even if your woman says she wants you to. *Especially* when your woman says she wants you to.

Your woman will ask you to do all kinds of things, every day. Do not allow yourself to be swayed from your truth, from the direction of your heart. Underneath your woman's superficial request is her actual desire and need: she wants your passionate fullness to pervade her, she wants to be able to trust the unshakability of your loving, she wants to feel in her bones that your divine masculine presence is stronger than your distractibility.

Your woman is a form of the goddess, taunting you, testing you, seducing you, ready to chop your head off with her wrath if you are weak and ambiguous in your truth, and ready to surrender to the force of your loving if you are steady and brilliant in your loving consciousness.

Know that your woman is always pleased most by your strength in love, freedom, and consciousness. If her requests and desires can sway you from what she knows is your highest goal, she will be angry and disappointed with you, even though she asked for it. Always act to maintain your fullest consciousness. Always apply your sword of discrimination to your woman's requests, never taking them at face value, but always checking with your deepest wisdom and following the road of your highest truth, even if it seems to mean disappointing your woman. She won't be disappointed if she feels you are strong and clear in the true direction of your heart. And if she *is* disappointed by your deepest truth, you shouldn't be with her. ◆

31

Her Complaint
Is Content-Free

*Women are always wanting divine masculine
presence in a man, regardless of their specific
complaint or mood. A man should hear his
woman's complaints like warning bells, and then do
his best to align his life with his truth and purpose.
However, if he believes in the literal content of her
complaint, he will immediately go off course, for
the content reflects her present mood more than a
careful observation of his tendencies over time. Her
complaint should be valued as a reminder to "get it
together," and perhaps as an indication as to how.
But more often than not, the specifics of her
complaint do not describe the real, underlying
action or tendency that needs to be changed.*

Your woman says, "How can you spend so much time in front of the
TV when our rent is due in a few days, we're behind on car pay-
ments and you just lost your job?"

"Don't worry about it, I have a job interview tomorrow."

"Well, why don't you get off your butt! You said you were going to
clean out the garage weeks ago. I can hardly get to the car!"

"OK. OK. I'll clean the garage this afternoon."

Your woman stops talking and goes about her business, but you can feel her simmering anger and tension. You don't like to be around her when she's like this. You want to get out of the house.

"I'll be back in a few hours and I'll clean the garage," you say, as you grab your coat and head for the door.

You hear a glass break in the kitchen, so you go in and find your wife furious. "I can't take this any more!" she wails.

"What? I said I'd clean the garage. What's going on?" you wonder.

"I just can't take it!" she cries out, pulling away from you, closing up, and not letting you touch her.

"I don't get it. I said I'd clean the garage. I have a job interview tomorrow. Everything is going to be fine. What do you want?"

You've probably had some version of this conversation with your woman. It holds a key to masculine growth in freedom. And it reveals a common mistake men make with their women.

The thing your woman is complaining about is rarely the thing she is complaining about. It is a mistake to believe the content of what she is saying, and then respond to her complaints, point by point. When she complains about financial issues, she is usually feeling a lack in your masculine capacity to direct your life with clarity, purpose, integrity, and wisdom. The money itself is secondary. If you were poor but totally conscious, happy, full of integrity, fearless, humorous, loving and giving your fullest gift to the world and to your woman, she wouldn't complain about lack of money.

When you say you will clean the garage, and then weeks pass and you haven't, her complaint isn't really about the garage. Sure she'd like a clean garage, but this is a superficial issue. The deeper issue is that you didn't do what you said you would. You gave her your word, and you didn't follow through. She can't trust what you say. And this hurts her, deeply.

She might seem to be overreacting to you. Why is she so hysterical? It's only a garage. But she can feel your lack of integrity. Not having cleaned the garage yet seems like a small thing to you, but it shows you don't follow through with your word, with your purpose.

Your word is a demonstration of your purpose, of your masculine core. When you don't follow through with what you say you are going to do, she feels that your masculine core is weak. She feels let down. She can't trust your masculine direction. And so she feels a great loss. Over time, she will begin to build up her own masculine protection against your lack of integrity. She will begin to guard herself against the hurt that your lack of carry-through causes. She will harden herself, becoming angular and tense. To you, the garage seems trivial. To her, you have failed at your word. She can't trust you.

It's very much as if your woman were to become slovenly. The core of the feminine is energy or radiance. If she stops taking care of herself, if she becomes dull and drab, always tired and worn out, then she is unable to give you the feminine energy you desire in intimacy. You might still love her, but you will begin to look elsewhere for feminine energy.

At the level of polarity, you are attracted to an enlivened by her feminine radiance. Likewise, at the level of polarity, she is attracted to and relaxed by your masculine clarity, direction, integrity, and presence. When she complains about you watching TV, it is usually more a complaint about your whole life, your lack of persistence and clarity. If your woman felt you were living totally in your clarity of purpose, if she felt you totally present with her when you chose to be with her, then you said, "I'm going to relax and watch TV for half an hour," it would be fine. It's not the TV watching itself that really bothers her, although that is what she'll talk about.

You must listen to your woman more as an oracle than as an advisor. She usually is speaking in a very tangential, but revelatory, style. She is revealing your unconscious habits that prevent your fullest awakening in consciousness. Your unconsciousness causes her pain. She won't say it that way, but that's what she is indicating.

Don't argue with her about the garage and the job interview. That's not what she's talking about, even though that's what she's talking about. Hear her complaint as the universe giving you signs about your life. Is watching TV right now the best way to use the moment? Sometimes you need the recreation, but sometimes you are just being lazy, trying to forget the responsibilities you have created in your life.

Did you purposefully lie to your woman about cleaning the garage? Or did you just let it slide, like you do with so many commitments you make in your life? Can you really blame your woman for being hurt by the lack of integrity that shows in your life?

If she can't trust you with living *your* life from your deepest wisdom and fullest capacity, she can't trust you with *her* life. She can't trust your masculine impeccability, so she naturally will compensate by overdeveloping her own. She is not only being masculine for herself, now she's being masculine for you. If she's got to remind you of the job interview or the mess in the garage, she's supplying the masculine direction for the both of you. And this results in stress. Her body will begin to show it. She will become less radiant and less relaxed in her feminine power and glory because she has to compensate for your failure.

The bags under your woman's eyes and the lines in her face may reveal much about how clearly you are living your highest purpose. Of course, your woman has her own unconscious habits to outgrow; but sometimes she is reflecting yours. Try to do your best to determine which of her "problems" are actually exquisitely sensitive bodily feedback to the way you are living your life. You know the amount of bullshit you are kidding yourself with. So does she. It just hurts her more than it does you. ◆

32

She Doesn't Really Want to Be Number One

A woman sometimes seems to want to be the most important thing in her man's life. However, if she is the most important thing, then she feels her man has made her the number one priority and is not fully dedicated or directed to divine growth and service. She will feel her man's dependence on her for his happiness, and this will make her feel smothered by his neediness and clinging. A woman really wants her man to be totally dedicated to his highest purpose—and also to love her fully. Although she would never admit it, she wants to feel that her man would be willing to sacrifice their relationship for the sake of his highest purpose.

Imagine that a man must go off to war. He hugs his woman good-bye. She is crying.

"Please don't go," she begs.

"You know that I must," he answers.

They look each other deeply in the eyes.

"You know that I love you," he says to her.

"Yes. I know. And I also know you must go," she replies, and another gush of tears bursts from her heartbroken face.

He turns and walks out the door, to his necessary destiny, as his woman, full of pain and pride, watches him disappear.

This exaggeratedly dramatic scene captures a profound energetic principle: Although your woman seems to want to be the most important thing in your life, she actually can trust and love you more if she is not.

A man's highest purpose is his priority, not his intimacy. Your woman knows this. Deep inside, she really wants it to be this way. The woman in the scene above would actually feel strange if her man suddenly said, "I've changed my mind. You are more important to me than the freedom of mankind. You are the most important thing in my life, and I don't care if my service to humanity is needed elsewhere, so I'm staying here with you." Even though part of her would feel glad, a deeper part of her would feel deflated, emptied, let down.

And yet, as her man leaves the door to accomplish his mission, she cries, wishing he didn't have to go. But he does have to go. And she knows it.

If a woman has become the point of your life, you are lost. You have a gift to give, a purpose to fulfill, a deep heart-impulse that moves you. If you have lost touch with this impulse, then you will begin to feel ambiguous in your life. You will make decisions because you have to, but they won't be guided by a deeper sense of purpose. You may take on your woman's purposes because they are stronger than yours. You may adapt your need for direction to externally regulated purposes, becoming a cogwheel company man or a dead-ended husband and parent, without leaving yourself open to your own greatest vision.

Be careful not to substitute default responsibilities for true purpose. It is easy to fill your day with chores and obligations, coming up for air only long enough to watch some TV or have quick sex. It's also easy to give up entirely on living a life of absolute commitment to truth, settling for the common life of absolute commitment to work, family, intimacy, and friends. Yet, you can only be a superior professional, father, husband, and friend when you are living these relationships as gifts given from your core, not as what's left over because you don't have the guts to discover your core impulse and live on its basis.

If you aren't living from your core, giving your fullest gifts, everyone will feel your lack of true purpose. Your kids will challenge your authority. Your colleagues will take advantage of you. Your friends won't expect much of you. And your wife won't trust you.

Even though she may seem to want to be the center of your life, she doesn't. She wants you to *know* the center of your life, however, so she can trust you. Even if you must go off somewhere without her to fulfill your purpose, like a man going to war, she will be able to trust you and love you, as long as your purpose is real and true.

If you are always watching TV, reading magazines, or gambling, your woman will feel your trivialization of life. She will feel you settling for less, and will resent the frivolity of your will.

But if you have discovered the purpose springing from your deepest core, and if your entire life is aligned by this deep purpose, your woman will feel the truth of your choices. Though she may not always *like* your choices, she will *love* them, and she will love you for having the courage to live your truth. She can relax and trust you because, even if you are enjoying watching TV, reading magazines, and gambling now and then, she knows that you would never compromise your highest purpose in life—which includes, but is not centered nor dependent on, your relationship with her. ◆

33

Your Excellent Track Record Is Meaningless to Her

A man's track record means nothing to the feminine. A man could be perfect for ten years, but if he's an asshole for 30 seconds his woman acts like he's always been one. The feminine responds to the moment of energy, forgetting her man's history of past behavior. A man's past behavior is irrelevant to his woman's feeling in the moment. But men base much on another man's history of behavior, so they think their own track record should count for something. But to a woman, it doesn't.

It's been a tough and late day at work. You finally come home, and your woman is upset. You forgot that you were supposed to have dinner with another couple that night, and the time has passed. Your woman is furious.

"I'm sorry I'm late, but this was an unusual day," you say. "I haven't worked late for months, but I had to today. You probably can't even remember the last time I forgot a date together we had planned. I hardly ever forget those kinds of things."

"Well, you did today. And that's what counts."

There is no use trying to mitigate her anger by referring to your great track record. To the feminine, history is irrelevant. What counts is the feeling in the moment. If you let her down now, it doesn't matter that you haven't let her down for months, or even years. Your past successes mean nothing to her present feeling of your failure.

For you as a man, it is probably easier to forgive and forget an occasional mistake made by another man who has a great track record. What pisses you off is when a man lacks integrity and continually fails at his word. But even big mistakes are fairly easy to let go of when made by a man who is otherwise impeccable. You know he really does the best, and this mistake was a rare exception.

But, for the feminine, the past is entirely irrelevant. One wrong word in the midst of a five hour lovemaking session that was otherwise perfect could collapse your woman as completely as if you had spent two hours making mistakes.

Instead of getting angry because she's so upset that you made one little mistake in a long series of successes, instantly shift the energy between you. Remember, history is irrelevant to the feminine, so your mistake is as easily forgotten as your successes. As soon as you see she's upset, immediately assume happiness. Shock her with your love. Make her smile and laugh with your humor. Lick her neck, or lift her off the ground and pretend you're King Kong. Surprise her in some loving way, and the emotional slate will be wiped clean. Your momentary failure will be effectively vanished, as irrelevant as the long line of your successes.

Restore love and happiness in the present moment, don't justify your little mistake by referring to your long line of successes. ◆

34

She Wants to Relax in the Demonstration of Your Direction

A woman must be able to trust you to take charge
if she relaxes her own masculine edge. This is true
financially, sexually, emotionally, and spiritually.
The man doesn't have to actually do all the work,
but he must be able to steer the course if his woman is
going to relax into her feminine without fear.

Some women want to be in charge most of the time. This desire to guide direction—handling the remote control for the TV or choosing the city in which to live—is a masculine desire, in men and women. If your woman has a more masculine sexual essence, she will prefer to be in charge of the direction of your lives most of the time.

But if your woman has a feminine sexual essence, there will be times that she would like to pleasurably relax and let go of being in charge. She would like to relax in her feminine and let you make the decisions. If you are not able to take charge, if you don't know the direction you want to go, your woman will feel you floundering. She will have to take charge again, since you are unable. She won't be able to relax.

The more relaxed she is in her feminine, the more radiant your woman will be. You have probably noticed that your woman's radiance can change instantly. One moment she might seem dull and weary. Then, perhaps after you praise her or surprise her with a gift of love, suddenly she is glowing. She looks 15 years younger. The lines in her face have disappeared in seconds.

If you want your woman to be able to relax into her feminine and shine her natural radiance, then you must relieve her of the necessity to be in charge. This doesn't mean you need to boss her around. It means you need to know where you are heading and how you are going to get there, in every way, including financially and spiritually.

If you have the slightest uncertainty or ambiguity about your financial future, your woman will feel it. You don't have to say anything about it. She'll feel your doubt or ambiguity in your body, eyes, and the tone of your voice. It's not that you have to make a lot of money; you just have to be responsible for your finances and take your future into account. You might choose to be a monk; what's important is that you are clear, accountable, and directed from your deepest core of wisdom. Then, your woman can relax. She knows where you stand and what your plans are. She can feel your integrity. She can trust your direction, because she knows it comes from your deepest core. She is not swimming in the air of your uncertainty but standing on solid ground, the ground that you've provided by your clarity.

Even more important is your spiritual direction. Where is your relationship going? What are your lives about? What does it all add up to? How will the two of you continue to grow without getting stuck in the ruts of mediocrity?

If your woman feels that you have lost your spiritual direction, she will seek direction herself and attempt to impose it on you, since you don't seem to have any yourself. If she feels that you are totally absorbed in your work, for instance, and when you're not obsessing about your career you are absorbed in TV, then she will wonder, "Is this it? Is this what our relationship amounts to? Is this the highest vision that my man sees?" If she feels you lacking in your financial clarity or your spiritual clarity, she will not be able to relax with you. She will automatically begin directing her own life, and probably yours too. She will develop her own masculine direction, since you are lacking. And, by doing so, her radiance will diminish.

The more ambiguous you seem, financially and spiritually, the more she will need to pour her energy and attention into her own masculine direction and goals. For some women, this is great; they need to develop their own masculine energy. Other women, however, have already developed their masculine. They would like the opportunity to relax their own masculine and receive yours as a gift. How can you tell if your woman's self-direction is healthy for her? If she becomes more and more full and happy as she pursues her direction, then it is good for her. If she becomes more and more stressful, taut, and emotionally angular, then she is animating excess masculine direction. She is pushing herself in ways that may signal your irresponsibility.

How can you be more responsible? Not necessarily by doing more work. You become more responsible by knowing your deepest purpose, and then arranging your finances and spiritual life from that knowingness. For your woman to relax in her radiance and feminine happiness, she needs to feel that she can get on your train and that it's going exactly where she wants to go. It doesn't matter if your woman earns more or less money than you—or even if she earns all the money in the relationship. What matters is if she can feel your loving clarity, wisdom, and certainty of direction. As long as she can feel that you are taking the finances into account and arranging your lives together so that the deepest love and fullest gifts can manifest, she will be able to trust your masculine direction and relax in her feminine heart of radiance. ◆

PART

FIVE

Your Dark Side

35

You Are Always
Searching for Freedom

The essential masculine ecstasy is in the moment
of release from constraint. This could occur when
facing death and living through it, succeeding in
(and thus being released from) your purpose, and
in competition (which is ritual threat of death). The
masculine is always seeking release from constraint
into freedom. The feminine often doesn't understand
these masculine ways and needs.

Your basic motivation is to be released from constraint and experience the freedom on the other side. What are some of the most common forms of masculine ecstasy? Orgasm is one. The typical masculine orgasm, as you probably know, involves a build-up of tension, or constraint, until the dam finally breaks, and your tension and energy are released. The post-orgasmic state is one of death-like peace, an emptiness akin to a blissful oblivion. The masculine is always seeking this release in one way or another.

Most sports provide this masculine thrill of release from constraint into freedom. In football, for instance, the team with the ball is constrained by the other team that is lined up in front and ready to block them. The challenge is to break through the line and carry the ball to freedom. People with masculine essences become insanely emotional during this ritual of challenge and release from constraint into freedom. And if the freedom is achieved, men will shout and cheer, as if their deepest heart desire has occurred—and it has. This breakthrough into freedom, however it occurs, is the main motive of the masculine. All masculine goals—at work, on the meditation cushion, or on the football field—are directed toward more freedom.

The typical masculine desire for freedom involves the feeling of death, which is the ultimate masculine fear and freedom, in one way or another. Orgasm is actually called *petite mort* or "little death" in French. You say that you hope your favorite football team "kills" the other team, and you celebrate your financial "killings" with great glee.

You are probably also familiar with darker aspects of the masculine desire for freedom. War, which is motivated by the desire for freedom, is a quintessential masculine pursuit. Most sports are ritualized war, but actual war itself resonates with the core of most men. Even movies about war—men being at their edge, giving it all they've got, up against death itself, motivated by a higher cause—evoke intense emotion in men. The capacity to face death for the sake of freedom, whether actually in war or ritually on the football field or chess board, is the ultimate masculine act, evoking men's deepest emotions.

The same capacity to face death is necessary for spiritual freedom. To live free in spirit, you must be willing to face your fears and let go of anything that limits your love. The attachment to comfort and security is what limits most men in their capacity to make a spiritual touchdown. The other team is your own need for private security. You are fighting a war with your own self-sense. To be free is to die to your need to be a separate self. What, then, could be constrained? Ego death, absolute surrender to the point of oneness, is the ultimate freedom. Few men ever release themselves enough to relax in this depth of freedom because they are afraid of absolutely no stress. No stress means no thoughts, no sense of protected self, no mission to accomplish. The end of the masculine game.

Yet, this stress-free, unprotected end of the game is exactly what you are always seeking, through orgasm, financial killings, or winning a war. You are willing to experience lesser forms of masculine "death" and ecstasy, but you are unwilling to face the death of your separate self-sense, and finally *be* the freedom you have only allowed yourself to taste in moments.

Men will always enjoy facing forms of "death" and coming out the other side into freedom, whether in the form of boxing matches, cop movies, martial arts, orgasm, philosophy (the stress releasing "ah" of insight), or ego death. You must own the primacy of your desire to be free. Then, you can enjoy the lesser forms of masculine ecstasy, but dedicate yourself to its highest form: transcendence of the fear of death by facing the limiting stress of your own self-sense, and relaxing through it, into the absolute freedom you have always intuited at your core, but sought through only temporary means.

The feminine, on the other hand, is not seeking freedom, but love. A woman's bliss is not in emptiness, but in fullness. Her means is not release, but surrender. This is why a woman is upset when a man begins snoring after orgasm. He has finally achieved, in post-ejaculative emptiness, the blissful freedom from stress he has been seeking all day, one way or another. She, however, is hoping to experience love and fullness through sex, and a snoring man just doesn't do it for her.

The feminine seeks fullness and abhors emptiness. She will fill her empty shelves with knickknacks, seashells, and pebbles collected from special places. When she does not feel full of love, she seeks to fill herself with ice cream, chocolate, or conversation, rather than empty her stress through TV or ejaculation, as men often do. Her dark side enjoys the emotional aggression in soap operas and romance novels, rather than the physical aggression of boxing matches and porno movies. She longs to fill her sense of spiritual emptiness by surrendering her heart and being filled with love. Her basic means toward spiritual unity is surrender into the devotional fullness of unbounded love, rather then breaking through the fear of ego-death into the unconstrained infinity of absolute freedom.

In the end, the feminine search for love and the masculine search for freedom reach the same destination: the unbounded and infinite ground of being who you are, which is both absolute love and freedom. But until you finally relax into the place you always are, your woman will continue to surrender—to you, chocolate, and shopping—in the hope of being filled with love, and you will continue to release yourself—through television, orgasm, and financial success—in the hope of being emptied of stress into unconstrained freedom. ◆

36

Own Your
Darkest Desires

If a man disowns his dark masculine desire for
freedom, then he kinks the hose of his masculine
force. His energy will not flow freely, and his
attention will be bound by unfulfilled yearnings.
Most importantly, if his hose is kinked in this way,
he weakens his masculine capacity to stand fearless
in the death that is conscious life. He will not be
able to face the unknown, the groundless ground of
being, and still function from his heart in love.

When was the last time you really ravished your woman? That is, when was the last time you really "took" her, savagely, lovingly, with no inhibition whatsoever? Or, has it been so long that you are fascinated and even turned on by rape scenes on TV or in the movies?

When you are unable to express your dark passions with love, then they go underground in your psyche. Your dark desires become disconnected from your heart. Instead of being moved to embrace your woman with masculine force and aggressive passion—throwing her down on the bed, ripping off her clothes, and pinning her down beneath your body as you both yield yourselves in ecstatic loving—you begin to fantasize about controlling and dominating women in unloving ways.

The desire to ravish is the sexual aspect of the same masculine desire that wants to break through opponents on a basketball court, break through philosophical barriers to intellectual insight, or break through the fear of death into spiritual freedom. The desire to ravish is the desire to break through a woman's resistances to open her heart and body into ecstatic loving. The pleasure is in releasing her from all the conventional restraints of her psyche, so she has no choice but to surrender in love.

When this masculine desire to ravish becomes dissociated from your heart, then you will settle for breaking through a woman's resistance without love, through violence or coercion. Although few men will readily admit it, most men have entertained fantasies about forcing a woman to have sex against her will. In fact, most women have entertained fantasies of being forced to have sex against their will. The dark feminine desire, to be forced to surrender, is as strong as the dark masculine desire to penetrate through a woman's resistance. The difference between rape and ravishment is love.

Your woman surrendering to receive your strong love, or you lovingly "forcing" your woman to surrender into greater ecstasy, is the basis of ravishment. When you are unwilling to play these dark masculine and feminine poles in love and humor, then they will appear in loveless ways, such as rape fantasies, obsessions with soap operas, tragic stories of loss and brutality, and violent pornography.

Sexual energy is at the root of your bodily force of life, and your relationship to ravishment reveals your relationship to life altogether. This is also true of your woman. If your woman is afraid to surrender completely and receive your loving in all of her parts, she will also be afraid to surrender completely and receive the loving of the divine through and through her. She will feel essentially empty, and so seek to be filled with the "love" of food, shopping, social events, and conversation.

If you are afraid to yield yourself completely in the ecstasy of physical love with your woman—going beyond all sense of control and separate self so your heart and her heart are one in the midst of absolutely abandoned passion—then you will also be afraid to yield yourself completely in divine freedom. You will grasp onto your sense of self and control instead of yielding through your fear into the boundless unknowable infinity of existence. You will feel full of your own tension, and so attempt to empty yourself in the conventional masculine habits of TV, ejaculation, and work.

You must learn to let go, absolutely, in love with your woman. Unless you choose to live your life as a celibate, there is no way around this. You must be as fearless with your sexual desire as you are with your spiritual desire. The essential masculine fear is loss of self—which is also the essential masculine desire. So, if you are like most men, you are willing to lose your self in controllable ways like sports, newspapers, and orgasm, but you remain fearful of losing your self, for real, in love-ecstasy with your woman, surrendered in the unknowable infinity beyond mind.

As an experiment, the next time you make love with your woman, feel through your own physical and emotional boundaries into her. Feel into her so deeply that you become unaware of yourself and totally aware of her. Feel yourself move into her, your boundaries dissolving so that you become her, utterly aware of her breath, her movements, her emotions. Love her with more abandon than you've ever allowed yourself before. Feel through not only your boundaries, but also her boundaries, so that you are both dissolved in the immense force of your loving. Relax into the force of love so completely that only love remains.

Allow this love to ravish your woman to bursting, filling her heart and body beyond capacity, so she has no choice but to surrender to the depth and force of your loving. With a relaxed and spontaneous body, allow your love to penetrate her so deeply that she is overwhelmed, to the point of tears, as you yield yourself, letting go of all fear, only giving love.

In the midst of this self-yielding and giving of love, allow your entire masculine desire to manifest, dark and light. Do and be everything you ever wanted with her, in love, spontaneously, and with deep feeling into her and through her. From time to time, take special care to allow space for her energies and desires to take you to places you would never have gone on your own.

By reclaiming the full force of your dark masculine loving, you will not only re-own your capacity to ravish your woman in selfless ecstasy, but you will also re-own your spiritual guts. You will develop the courage to let go of yourself in the face of ego-death. You will unkink the hose of your masculine spiritual force by opening to the dark side of your sexual desiring, allowing the force of love itself to draw you beyond the need for control and fearful grasping. You will cultivate your capacity to "die" into love, with no need to hold onto your self.

Over time, as this force moves through you more freely, you will discover a naturally enhanced capacity to yield into spiritual "death," or the dissolution of your sense of separate self in the freedom of unboundedness. Rather than gripping onto yourself, you will be able to ease yourself more fully into the consciousness who you truly are, and in doing so you will recognize the Great One, with no boundaries, who is living you now, and who is not other than you. But to let go of your sense of individuated separate self takes guts. And you won't have them if you don't even have the daring to let go of the sense of separation between you and your woman while making love.

To truly ravish your woman in love, you must yield yourself in the worship and trust of her heart, which, in truth, is your heart. Such fearlessness will prepare you for and perhaps even initiate you into the worship and trust of consciousness itself, such that you will find greater and greater capacity to yield into and as the boundless One who you truly are. ◆

37

She Wants the
"Killer" in You

*Among many other qualities, a woman wants
the "killer" in her man. She is turned off if her
man is afraid and wants her to kill the cockroach
or the mouse while he stands on a chair and
watches. She is turned off if her man wants her to
get out of bed in order to check out the strange
sounds in the house to find out if a burglar
made the noise. Fearlessness, or the capacity to
transcend the fear of death for the sake of love, is a
quintessential form of the ultimate masculine gift.*

▼
Although your woman doesn't want you to be a killer, she is turned
on by your capacity to kill. And, she is turned off by your lack of
this capacity. For instance, imagine that a big cockroach crawls into the
living room. You jump on the couch and scream to your woman, "Kill it,
please, kill it!" She would probably not be turned on.

Or, imagine that you are in bed with your woman at night. You hear
some strange noises downstairs in the kitchen. You are afraid. So, you ask
your woman to go down and check it out. She is not going to become
excited by your masculine valiancy.

In both of these cases, your woman will feel your fear. She doesn't want
you to be a killer, but she does want to feel that you are capable of facing
death, if necessary. In fact, she wants to feel you are capable of killing, if

necessary. If an insane maniac broke into your home and was about to murder your children, your woman would not be particularly happy if you had the opportunity to do something about it but instead you said, "Well, OK, Mr. Maniac, whatever you want to do is fine with me."

The dark masculine energy of the warrior, the one who could face death and kill when necessary, is an essential part of you. Today's current fashion is to suppress both the dark masculine and the dark feminine, so we have a large population of wimpy men and polite women. But beneath the nice veneer of most women lies the wrathful goddess who would chop the head off of every mediocre "new age" man. And beneath the patient smile of most men lies the warrior of love who would ravish his woman into bliss rather than listen to her chat in pointless emotional circles.

But the dark masculine energy has been suppressed so thoroughly these days that the ordinary man would prefer to paste a smile on his bored face, rather than penetrate his woman's tension with uncompromising love. And he's just as cautious about disrupting his own well-planned life of comfort and security in order to penetrate his own fear of death.

Although she may resist it at first, your woman, if she has a feminine sexual essence, wants to feel your fearlessness. She wants to feel your capacity to face her closure, anger, and tension, without trying to minimize her feminine force. She wants to feel your persistence in loving, so that her fury cannot turn you away. She wants to feel your capacity to stand strong in your own desires and ravish her because you love her, unafraid of her dark energy.

She wants to feel this dark masculine capacity not simply because she wants to be ravished, but because it is a sign of your overall capacity to face and know death, your own and others'. And it is this capacity that makes you trustable as a man, both as a human warrior and as a spiritual warrior. The knowledge of death makes you humble and courageous. The knowledge of death strips the armor from your heart and allows the knowledge of love. This knowledge of death and love is your doorway through your own fears, through your own clinging to security, and into the unknowable mystery that lies beyond your little cell of self-protected importance.

Your woman's desire for your dark side, in love, is a gift to you. By honoring her desire through the cultivation of your dark and fearless loving, your need for self-protection will decrease, and every moment will stand more naked, vulnerable, and true, released of your need for consolation and false self-assurance. Rather than smiling at your present experience from behind a curtain of safety, minimizing your participation with the always life-threatening potential of the moment, you will lovingly surrender your position and ravish the moment, penetrate to its core, and find yourself identical to it. Feeling through and through and through is your only freedom.

The "killer" your woman wants is the one who knows that life is a process of dying through to that which cannot be lost. Only in this sacrifice of fear can your heart remain unguarded. Facing the potential burglar at night is only a sign to your woman that you are willing to lose everything into love. ◆

38

She Needs Your Consciousness to Match Her Energy

A man must be able to meet his woman with consciousness equivalent to her energy. The feminine destructress must be met by the masculine destroyer. The goddess of devotion must be met by the god of all-pervading love. Dark or light, a man can't be stuck in, or avoid, any areas of his masculine capacity or his woman will test him there. These areas of testing are usually first on the dark side. Only after trust is established there, only when the dark feminine lover knows she will be met by the dark masculine lover, will testing proceed toward the light.

As you probably know, your woman is capable of being a witch, a sex slave, an Amazon, a goddess of light, a nurturing mother, a demoness, a luscious lover, a wise teacher, a wild animal, and everything in between. As a general rule, she will keep returning to the energy that you cannot match.

For instance, if you are particularly turned off by her anger, she will seem to return, again and again, to the energy of anger. If you are unable to embrace her anger in the ferocity of your loving, transforming her anger into passion, she will continue to test your capacity to do so. Any of her energies that you are unable to transform into love through the force, clarity, and humor of your consciousness will return for you to face, again and again.

Perhaps she gets tense and agitated often. You have tried talking about this with her countless times. Nothing seems to make a difference. So you just stop trying. You learn to tolerate her tension.

Without consciously choosing to get tense, she will continue to test you. Until your consciousness is able to blossom her beyond her tension, you will be tested. A lesser man might decide, "Well, she's going to have to deal with it herself." But she would not be in relationship with you if she wanted to deal with it herself. She wants your consciousness—clear, strong, and free—as much as you want her radiance. If you are not penetrating her moods, she can't feel your free consciousness. Instead, she feels you throw up your hands, impotent in the face of her energy.

The secret is to match her energy with consciousness *demonstrated through your body*. If she is screaming and breaking dishes, your body must meet her energy. Your fearlessness and strength of love must manifest through your body. If you are cringing, if your voice is restrained, and you are telling her that you love her, she won't believe you. If you walk up to her, hold her in your arms, and laugh affectionately in the humor of the moment, she will feel your freedom, if it is for real. She will feel it because it is communicated through your body.

Your body, tone of voice, and the look in your eyes mean a lot more to her than anything you could say. Don't tell her what to do, but do it with her, with your body. If she is tense and closed down, lift her arms up above her head and kiss her heart. Don't just tell her to open up. Actually open her up, physically, with the openness of your body.

The same is true of her bliss; you must meet it bodily. If she is in the ecstatic throes of devotional surrender to divine love, then your consciousness must be just as free. Your body must meet hers full of relaxation, power, and trust. Your capacity to surrender through your fears and release your sense of separate self in divine communion must be as strong as her surrender into love. And you must show it through your body, not just your words.

If your surrender into communion is not as strong as hers, she will return to the place of your limiting fear, your weak link, and test you there. If you collapse or react with unlove when she questions your financial ability, she will continue to do so. If you feel weakened when she questions your sexual ability, she will continue to do so, implicitly or explicitly.

She will never trust your "lighter" masculine capacities until you have proven your "darker" masculine capacities. Your woman has an intuitive knowledge concerning your consciousness. She knows that if you are not free to meet her dark destructress energy and ravish her in love, you won't be free to meet the dark destructress of the world—who will challenge your spiritual freedom—with strength and love.

You need not concern yourself with pleasing her. That's not the point. She is offering you a gift. She is presenting you with an energy in the form of her mood and emotion, offering you an opportunity to learn to "master" this energy with your fearless loving. Whatever energy she offers you, you can be sure the world will offer it to you as well. If you have ever tried to increase your income, or magnify your spiritual clarity, you know that the world will test you. Only through your persistence, fearlessness, and loving service does the world yield to your efforts.

And the same is true of your woman. You are not trying to please her. You are learning to pervade the world, including her, with consciousness and love. That is what you are here to do.

The world will test you with dark, wild, and resistive energies financially and spiritually, for example, in the same way your woman is testing you emotionally. If you hide your deepest gifts from her in fear, you will also hide your deepest gifts from the world in fear. If you give up at a certain point with her, you will likewise only go so far in the giving of your gift to the world.

Your woman knows your weaknesses better than anybody. She knows where you will falter and give up. She knows the degree of mediocrity you will settle for. And, she knows your true capacity as a full man, a man of free consciousness and love. Her gift, if she is a good woman, is to test you with her darkest moods, over and over and over, until your consciousness is unperturbed by feminine challenge, and you are able to pervade her with your love, just as you are here to pervade the world. In response to your fearless consciousness, she will drench your world in love and light. ◆

PART

*Feminine
Attractiveness*

39

The Feminine
Is Abundant

There is never a shortage of women or
feminine energy. If a man feels that there aren't
enough women, or that life isn't giving him what
he wants, he is simply negating his relationship to
the feminine. This sense of starvation—"life is not
sustaining me" or "there are no good women"—is
usually rooted in a man's early childhood relationship
with his mother. Life itself is the feminine. There is
never a shortage of feminine energy, only a resistance
to receiving, trusting, and embracing it.

You must actually refuse feminine energy in order to feel tired, dry, and hungry for a woman. You are living in an ocean of feminine energy right now. Feminine energy is filling your body with life, beating your heart, and breathing your breath. There are women all around you who, with the proper initiation into mutually surrendered loving, would feed every cell of your body with juicy, enlivening, rejuvenative feminine energy. If you feel stranded on your own masculine island of weariness and hunger, it is because you are refusing to embrace the energy and women around you.

Whenever you are feeling isolated and weary, feel the present moment as if it were a woman. Feel like you are embracing a woman, physically. Feel the front of your body as if it were pressed against the front of a woman's naked body, being filled with the delight of her feminine softness and liveliness. Feel her breasts and belly against you. Breathe deeply as if you were inhaling her intoxicating fragrance. And, while inhaling, receive deeply into your body not just her scent, but the very essence of feminine deliciousness, as if it were nourishing food for your masculine soul.

Relax your body and feel the ocean of feminine energy around you. Feel your surroundings as her form, the sounds around you as her moans and laughter, and the light around you as her smile. Actually relax with the moment as you would relax with your lover, not metaphorically but literally, bodily, with full intention and presence.

Do the same in the company of human women. Feel them not merely as friends, coworkers, or sisters, but as walking blessings of energy. Receive their anger as a jolt of awakening energy. Receive their sexiness as a blessing of enlivenment. Receive their happiness, even when you are depressed, as a light shower of refreshment. Open your breath and body and fully receive each woman's unique flavor of feminine energy, so your day becomes a feast of plenty.

You need not show the women you meet throughout the day that you are doing anything special at all. Continue to treat them in whatever way is appropriate for the situation. But through it all, relax and enjoy the bountifulness of feminine energy that surrounds you, both in the form of human women and in the form of the moment together. ◆

40
Allow Older Women Their Magic

Men should support older women in their wisdom, power, and intuitive and healing capacities. Men should not degrade older women by demanding or desiring them to be like young women. There should be no such comparison. Each age of woman has its own value, and the transition from superficial shine to deep radiance is inevitable.

For many reasons, from biological to yogic, you are probably more sexually attracted to young women than older ones. Walking down the beach or street, your head is more likely to turn for a twenty year old woman than a sixty year old. This is quite natural.

But there is more to feminine energy than this. Youthful sexual attractiveness is a temporary aspect of a much deeper and more fundamental quality of feminine energy: radiance. Feminine radiance is not only the flush of a young woman's cheeks or the glow of her skin, but is the shine of life force itself. A woman's true radiance reveals the degree to which she is open, trusting, connected, and loving. Her capacity to love, in turn, allows her body to be moved by the power of life force itself. Herein lies the true nature of feminine radiance and power, far beyond the simple sexiness of a naive young woman.

When a woman is young, her body more easily conducts life force, and so she appears more radiant, in general, than an older woman. But even amongst young women there are those who are pretty just on the outside, and those whose beauty springs from their depths. As a woman ages, her skin begins to lose its youthful capacity to conduct life force. What remains obvious of her feminine radiance is primarily her beauty of depth.

In fact, it is this deep beauty that you find most attractive even in young women. There is a difference between your knee-jerk response to a cute babe and the open-hearted awe and mindless swoon you feel in the company of a woman who moves, breathes, smiles, and shines radiant feminine energy like a goddess. When looking into such a woman's eyes, you feel an almost breathtaking depth of compassion, love, and mystery. This deep feminine beauty or radiance need not be diminished by age. Actually, it can be magnified, deepened, and glorified.

If you are disconnected from your deep masculine core of purpose and consciousness, then you will also be disconnected from a woman's depth. You will see only skin deep, and you will be attracted to the superficial display of a woman's radiance, which often disappears with the passing of youth. You will inadvertently dishonor the true and deep forms of feminine radiance, and so contribute to the social cult of youth, wherein women try to look and behave younger—and more superficial—than they truly are, denying the power and radiance springing from their depths.

The natural sexiness of a young woman will always give you energy. You never need to deny this. But the awesome beauty and radiant ease of a deep woman can stop your mind, widen your heart, and suspend your body in the mystery of feminine grace, all in an instant, with a single gaze or touch, regardless of her body's age. And in relationship with such a woman, there are no bounds to the rapture which may resonate through your union. Boundless feminine love-radiance and temporary physical sexiness are both blessings; you must decide, moment by moment, and year by year, which qualities you will invoke and venerate with your attention, praise, and union.

As a woman grows older with wisdom, her "psychic weight" increases. She becomes a "bigger" woman, able to influence her surroundings with stronger magic than a less developed woman. She is able to read the signs of nature with great accuracy, as well as sway events with almost shocking reign. A superior man honors and appreciates this kind of magic, and knows that it complements his masculine style of accomplishment.

An older woman will also tolerate less of your bullshit than a younger woman. Although this might be one of your reasons for preferring younger women, you must choose your priority. If you find yourself attracted to younger women, be careful that you aren't trying to find an easy relationship with a woman who will let you slide. If your purpose is to become ever more free of your self-burdens and give your true gift to the world, then a spiritually mature woman—who won't let you slather in your comfy habits of security and distraction—may be an excellent ally for your journey. ◆

41

Turn Your Lust
Into Gifts

When a man sees a beautiful woman it is natural
for him to feel energy in his body, which he usually
interprets as sexual desire. Rather than dispersing
this energy in mental fantasy, a man should learn to
circulate his heightened energy. He should breathe fully,
circulating the energy fully throughout his body. He
should treat his heightened energy as a gift which could
heal and rejuvenate his body, and, through his service,
heal the world. Through these means, his desire is
converted into fullness of heart. His lust is converted into
service. His desire is not converted by denying sexual
attraction, but by enjoying it fully, circulating it through
his body (without allowing it to stagnate as mental
fantasy), and returning it to the world, from his heart.

▼

If you are like most men, sexual energy tends to go directly to one of two places. Either your head becomes stimulated and you fantasize about being with a woman who turns you on, or your genitals become stimulated in lustful need. Your head and genitals, however, are just the north and south poles of the whole body. A superior man circulates the energy of arousal throughout his body, taking particular care not to let it stagnate in swollen fantasies or appendages.

The purpose of sexual desire is creation. Reproduction is but the biological aspect of creation. As a man, you probably have much more to give the world than your children. Just as beautiful women inspire biological procreation, they also inspire artistic, social, and spiritual creativity. When it comes down to it, most creative men will admit that, one way or another, women are their muse and inspiration. Women bring them into the world. Women move them to create and serve humanity. In fact, some men would go so far as to say that, if it weren't for women, they wouldn't be interested in the world much at all.

If you are a man, you have probably found yourself inspired at some time or another by a woman. Such inspiration is usually temporary, because most men don't know how to cultivate their relationship to the feminine. They tend to be inspired, and then spurt it out, through spasms of thought and ejaculation. Then they seek inspiration again, through more women, or through other feminine sources, such as alcohol, drugs, or nature.

But if you learn to discipline your habits of building up and releasing mental and sexual tension, you can continually cultivate and magnify your inspiration. You can wean yourself from the addictive cycles of sexuality and intoxication. You can make use of the native force of sexual desire, for your woman and for other women, and convert your tendency toward fantasy and lust into the force of inspiration.

Feel lust. Feel what it really is, in its totality. Your lust reveals your real desire to unite with the feminine, to penetrate as deeply as possible, to receive her delicious light as radiant food for your masculine soul, and to give her your entirety, losing yourself in the giving, so that you are both liberated beyond your selves in the explosion of your gifts.

This explosion of gifting could be the basis of your life, not just a moment of sexual yielding. When you feel sexual lust or desire for any woman, breathe deeply and allow the feeling of desire to magnify. And allow it to magnify more. Don't let the energy become lodged in your head or genitals, but circulate it throughout your body. Using your breath as the instrument of circulation, bathe every cell in the stimulated energy. Inhale it into your heart, and then feel outward from your heart, feeling the world as if it were your lover. With an exhale, move into the world and penetrate it, skillfully and spontaneously, opening it into love. Through these means, allow women's sexiness to help you discover and give your gift, rather than beguile you into cycles of stimulation and depletion. ◆

42

Never Allow Your Desire to Become Suppressed or Depolarized

When a man denies his desire for the feminine, either by choice or due to familiarity, it is a sign of his depolarization even toward the world. He may seek a mistress in order to re-invigorate him, but this is usually only a temporary and complicated solution, since it is only a matter of time before his mistress also becomes familiar, and thus tiresome. Any woman toward whom a man becomes depolarized will feel his rejection, disgust, and turning away. In response, she will become angry and destructive. Her "unhusbanded" energy will begin to move chaotically, becoming even self-destructive. A man has no excuse; he must cultivate a polarized relationship to his woman and his world if he is to remain in relationship with them.

You have a choice. You could choose to give your gift as a renunciate celibate, living with only the most minimal engagement with the world and women. Or, you could choose to engage the world and women fully, as a way of giving your gift. If you choose to engage the world and women fully, then you must maintain a certain degree of polarization or mutual attraction with them. Otherwise, you will begin to reject, resist, and resent the world and women, undermining your capacity to give your gift.

You've probably seen the face of your woman when you've gotten to the point of "putting up" with her, rather than permeating her. She begins to look haggard and drawn. Her long face bespeaks a heart and body unravished by the clarity and force of your masculine loving. She never seems really happy.

Eventually, her resentment turns inward, and disease symptoms begin to appear in her body. Her skin seems to wither before your eyes. You dislike her smell. As her frustration and negativity build, you become less attracted, which, of course, deprives her of even normal human affection. When things get really bad, she seems so ugly and dark that you are repulsed, and your complete withdrawal leaves her barren at her core. You may stay together because you love each other, but both of you are totally depolarized, more disgusted than turned on by each other.

During these times you probably also begin to feel the same disregard toward the world. Over time, you may begin to lose interest in your projects and career. You may consider changing jobs, or finding another woman. It seems that newness, in and of itself, will be more attractive and exciting than your worn-out woman and your droning career.

And you are right. A new woman and new work will excite you and cheer you up. And this is exactly what a mediocre man does: He stays with a woman and a project for as long as they interest him and turn him on. When the excitement seems to wear off, he moves on to another and then another hopeful source of polarity and excitement.

It is not time that kills delight, but familiarity, neutralization, and lack of purpose. Another man might find your woman to be quite a turn-on even though she seems old-shoe to you. It may not be your woman who has worn out, but your capacity for desire. You may feel like having as little to do with her as possible. But your lack of desire is only that: a lack of desire. You have spent so much time with your woman that you have "rubbed off" on each other, like two magnets that have demagnetized each other. Familiarity breeds depolarization, and depolarization breeds contempt amongst lovers.

Every moment you treat your woman as simply a childcare helper or a buddy, you are neutralizing the same sexual differences that would secretly attract you to your female babysitter or business acquaintance. Over time, you actually begin to behave more sexually neutral with your woman than you do with other women you meet throughout the day.

Chances are, your woman is more sensitive to sexual energy than you. She will probably feel the effects of this sexual neutralization, or depolarization, before you will. And when she does, her first reaction will be to feel rejected. Not in any big way, but in a small, constant way that undermines her feminine radiance. Even when she shines, you will treat her with more sexual neutrality than a woman on the bus. She will feel hurt and become darkened, and you will feel even less attracted to her.

Although both of you are playing into this downward spiral of endarkening depolarization, you must not blame her. A superior man always assumes complete responsibility, knowing that, ultimately, he has no control at all and everything is out of his hands. He acts with impeccable courage and persistence, expecting nothing but the inherent feeling of completeness he enjoys in the fullest giving of his gift.

When your woman is looking withdrawn, dark, or downright ugly, assume she is a goddess and needs your divine invasion of her heart and body. Notice your incipient feeling of disgust for her dark mood, and take utter responsibility for her transformation. You know how fully committed you could be to, say, finishing a project at work. Treat her mood with the same ferocity of intent. Her mood is your challenge.

Can you invade her body and heart with so much love and humor that she laughs, relaxes, and brightens, in spite of herself? Can you bring out the consort in her by treating her with the same teasing and sexually pregnant touch and gaze as you would your mistress?

You will not want to, that's for sure. When you are depolarized, the last thing you want to do is get it up for that potato. And yet, this is exactly what a superior man does, with his woman and his world. He knows that when things get dreary it is his own doing. He knows that he is only truly happy when giving his gift, fully and to the last drop. He knows that depolarization is a sign that he has ceased giving fully of himself, and so the world and his woman have ceased responding in fullness.

Sometimes you must move on, to another job or another woman. That's fine, if it is a true movement of growth: clear, empowering, and an aspect of the ongoing giving of your gift. But, more often than not, your first impulse to move on comes when you have ceased invading the moment with your fullest capacity to give and instead are droning along, coping rather than creating.

You can spend decades coping with a job before you realize that you've wasted much of your life. After just a few minutes of coping with your woman, however, she will show you her pain. Her face will show it to you. Her tone of voice will reveal it. Her seeming ugliness will reflect the collapse of her radiant core in response to your ambiguity of desire. Her dark mood is as ugly and repulsive to you as your ambiguity is to her.

It only takes a moment of meeting a real challenge to bring a man back to full purpose, an emergency or a threat that demands his best. And it only takes a moment of praise and deep appreciation to re-evoke a woman's radiance. It can happen to your woman at the grocery store or at the spa, when a man signals his appreciation. Or it can happen at the kitchen table with you.

Rather than deciding to move on because you are too weak to overcome your own neutralized lack of desire, try to take on the challenge of manifesting love in the dreary world and in your dreary woman. Use your body and mind to smithereen your woman's darkness into love. Even if she has yellow eyes and fangs, she still loves to dance. It's up to your freedom and strength of transmission whether she drains your energy, bites your wimbly head off, or surrenders to your fearless passion. ◆

43

Use Her Attractiveness as a Slingshot Through Appearance

*A good woman is a source of inspiration
and attraction into the world for a man. He
must never forget, however, that neither the
world nor his woman is the purpose of his
existence. His practice is always to feel through
women and the world, without suppression or
disdain, into their source or very nature. A man's
attraction to women must be converted from
attraction to women into attraction through women.
He must feel his desire without suppression, and
then feel through his desire into the source-energy
of desire. He must feel through her beauty, into
the very delight of which her beauty is but a ripple
and reminder. His whole relation to appearance
is epitomized in his relation to women, either as
obsession, distraction, or revelation.*

▼

In your worship of women, never forget that they die. In your enjoyment of pleasure and delight, never forget that your sensations and feelings are fleeting, and never absolutely enough. Women can attract you, heal you, and inspire your gifts, but they will never satisfy you absolutely. Never. And you know this.

This is why women are so frustrating to you. Their promise attracts you, in one way or another, perhaps many times a day. And yet, throughout your life, you have learned and will continue to learn that they cannot make good on the promise. The fulfillment that seems like a woman is actually unavailable in her form.

The play of your body wanting her body is the most obvious hoax of fulfillment. If you have ever gotten the woman you've wanted, you know that it's never as good as you hoped for, at least not for very long. And yet you continue to be attracted, over and over and over, to the same woman or to different women. It's all the same thing. You are deceived by the mirage of your own desire. You are deluded by your own excitement. Women are not to blame. They are to be cherished.

And felt through. To feel a woman, and be merely yanked by your desire for her form, is stupid. Bulls and houseflies are yanked by feminine forms and desire. It is an endless, stupid round of mirage, desire, and need. And yet, so much of your life goes to looking at, thinking about, and desiring women, it's not something that can simply be shucked. But it is something that can be felt through.

Like a slingshot, the momentum of your desire can be used to deliver you to the source that women only promise.

Women are the epitome of appearance, all appearance, everything around you, potential and actual. And like women, all appearance seems to promise you something you want. You want success from your job. You want love from your woman. You want pleasure from your body. You want obedience from your dog. When you don't get what you want—when you lose money, your woman hates you, your body is in pain, and your dog bites you—you are unhappy.

When you do get what you want, you are less unhappy.

You are least unhappy when you are relieved of the need to get anything at all from appearance. Just driving in your car, wanting nothing, watching the trees go by, can be an epiphany of perfection. Deep sleep, orgasm, a day of fishing, looking into an infant's eyes, these occasions can relax you from your search long enough to realize that you already have what you seek, that what appearances promise is a revelation of your own deep and inherently blissful nature.

You *are* that which you seek, but you have left your own deepness and are looking elsewhere. The stress of not finding it creates its own need to be released. And so the cycle continues. You are chasing your own tail, and much of the time that tail looks suspiciously like a woman.

But you need not stop chasing. Instead, chase. Allow yourself to feel how badly you want her. Feel how deep is the itch you want scratched. Feel the need that drives you, for most of your adult life, to yearn for a woman, in flesh or in fantasy. And discover what it is you really want. You've had tit. You've had pussy. You've had nurturing. You've had wild passion. And none of it lasted. It wasn't even that good as long as it did last. Your need is far deeper than any woman can provide. So what is it?

Your ultimate desire is for the union of consciousness with its own luminosity, wherein all appearance is recognized as your deep, blissful nature, and there is only One. Your desire for union with a woman is a stepped-down version of this ultimate spiritual need.

You can use your desire as a doorway to spiritual oneness. Magnify your desiring to the brink of madness. Sustain it with full breath, relaxed body, and open heart. Embrace your woman, if you have one, and *give her what you want from her*. Give it all to her. Give it away to her. Give her so much of what you want from her that you can't tell who is who, the chaser has become the tail, and all motion stops in the intensity of self-release. There is only One.

The very light of your consciousness shines as the world, and it is looking back at you, appearing as woman. She often appears as what you most fear and desire. She is the goddess, ready to fuck you, murder you, and enlighten you. Her appearance and your desire can be an endless drama of need, or they can merge, becoming a doorway to your divine source.

In a moment of attraction, let your desire feel to her, but don't stop there. Feel through her. Do this constantly. Feel through her body when you are having sex with her. Feel through her anger when she is raging at you. Feel through her darkness when she seems ugly. Feel through her beauty when she most attracts you. By feeling through all of her forms, the superior man is not distracted or obsessed. Rather, his attention feels through the mirage of other, and he is released of need in the revelation of oneness.

Desire can be a doorway to deep oneness. Sexual union is a fractal, or stepped-down, reflection of the ever-present wedding of consciousness and its inherent luminosity. The superior man embraces his woman as his own form. The revelation of deep oneness is love.

Women can seem to bring you to your true nature. Or they can seem to take you away from it. Each moment of appearance and of woman may be a distraction, an obsession, or a revelation. Notice the distractions—tits, ass, wealth, and fame—and practice the revelation of oneness by feeling through the distractions. Notice the obsessions—tits, ass, wealth, and fame—and practice the revelation of oneness by feeling through the obsessions. Practice it with your woman, for real. Bow down to her, and then bow down through her, into the deep which only seems to have been an other. ◆

PART

SEVEN

Body

Practices

44

Ejaculation Should Be Converted or Consciously Chosen

There are many physical and spiritual reasons why ejaculation should be converted into non-ejaculatory whole body, brain, and heart orgasms. But there are also relational reasons. When a man has no control over his ejaculation, he cannot meet his woman sexually or emotionally. She knows she can deplete him, weaken him, empty him of life force. She has won. When a man ejaculates easily, he creates ongoing distrust in his woman. At a subtle level, she feels he cannot be trusted. She, and the world, can deplete and depolarize him easily. This subtle distrust will pervade the relationship. She will not only doubt him, but actually act to undermine his actions in the world. By undermining him she demonstrates and tests his weakness, but she also hopes that through such tests he can learn to remain full.

You won't be willing to bypass ejaculation until you have experienced the much greater pleasures which lie beyond it. In the meantime, notice how you feel in the minutes and days following ejaculation. If you have accumulated a lot of tension in your daily life, ejaculation will afford you with temporary release and relaxation. But as you live your life with more and more true purpose, you won't accumulate so much tension during the day. Then, you will discover that ejaculation, for the most part, actually depletes and weakens you.

It feels great for a few moments, but the price you pay for the genital sneeze of ejaculation is a much higher level of mediocrity in your daily life. You will find that you just don't have the extra gusto necessary to live your life with utter impeccability. Excess ejaculations pave the road to living a good life, but not a great life.

In a subtle way, excess ejaculations will diminish your courage to take risks, professionally and spiritually. You will settle for doing enough to get by, to be comfortable, but you will find that you would rather watch TV than write your novel, meditate, or make that important phone call. You will have enough motivation to live a decent life, but ejaculations drain you of the "cutting through" energy that is necessary to pierce your own wall of lethargy and slice through the obstructions that arise in the world. Your gift will remain largely ungiven.

Your woman can feel all of this. She may be sexually turned on by making you ejaculate. It may please her in the short run. She may even say she feels sexually unfulfilled if you don't ejaculate. But there is also a deeper part of her that has never been sexually fulfilled by you because of your tendency to ejaculate frequently and soon.

Most women can experience many orgasms, and deeper and deeper orgasms. And more importantly, most women have a natural connection between their genitals and their heart. When you ejaculate and lose your erection, you are probably depriving your woman of her fullest capacity of heart reception and expression, which is evoked by relaxed, loving, watery hours of your fearless and unstressful genital penetration.

It is not simply your genital penetration that touches her deeply, though. The main penetration she feels is your yielding into her, through her, in love. It is the fullness of your presence, the actual invasion of her body by your consciousness, that most ravishes her.

Face it. If you are like most men, after an ejaculation or two you don't really want to penetrate or ravish her any more. You are content to relax in the emptiness of released tension. You don't feel much desire to enter your woman, bodily or emotionally, as you did just before you ejaculated.

Your woman feels your lack of desire. And she also intuits, perhaps subconsciously, that your lack of desire also applies toward the world. If she can drain you, so can the world. If she waits for your deepest gifts, as you lie feebly in the bed of undesire, so might the world. She senses that you have succumbed to her, that you have allowed temporary pleasures to diminish your capacity for fullest consciousness. She knows you will likewise succumb to the world.

One part of your woman is happy she made you come. She is happy you are relaxed and enjoying yourself. Another part of her is disappointed that you've allowed yourself to choose a temporary and pleasurable spasm over the endless ravishment of her and the world.

Sometimes she doesn't even know what she is missing. If she's never been with a man who has the capacity for full consciousness during sex, without conceding to the mechanical reflex of ejaculation, then she doesn't even know the extent of her capacity. She doesn't realize how deep and ecstatic sexual loving can be. She has never been utterly dissolved in loving. Surrendered beyond a shred of closure. Ravished through and through until there is nothing left to ravish. Just openness, love, radiant and alive, in all directions.

Some women, because of their need to guard and protect their wounded heart, would actually prefer that you ejaculate. That way, they never have to open all the way, or expose their depths to your touch. They know that after some oral sex and maybe a half-hour of intercourse, you will ejaculate, and it will be over. They don't want to feel you persist beyond their habitual closure. They would rather stay in control and draw out your ejaculation whenever they want.

It is especially this kind of woman who would most benefit from your undiminished capacity to lead her beyond all closure. And, it is especially with this kind of woman that you can cultivate your capacity to persist in the giving of your love. The world will constantly test your capacity to give your gift in the face of refusal. A woman who refuses your loving is simply a manifestation of this aspect of the world.

Deep down, your woman only wants love, as do you. Her refusal is a form of her fear. She may have childhood wounds that she is afraid of feeling. She may have been hurt as an adult and is afraid that if she opens she'll be hurt again. But in the present moment, all emotional resistance comes down to the same thing: a refusal to love.

Your masculine sexual gift is to coax, humor, shock, and caress her love into melting through her layers of fear. Without imposing your own needs on her, let your love penetrate to the deep part of her that is totally open to love, that is love itself, and coax it to the fore. Do this slowly, over time, not through conversation, but through bodily communicated presence, care, consciousness, and the liquid loving of sexual intermingling. When she feels the absolutely trustable nature of your loving—that you are truly with her, committed to loving, and you're not going to get lost in the self-enclosed spasm of your own pleasurizing—she will begin to trust you with her most vulnerable core.

But not until then. Every time she feels you contorting into your own sensations, she feels you "gone," not present, not trustable. She may enjoy giving you an ejaculation, but a deeper, perhaps unexpressed, part of herself will not trust you. Why should she? Why should she expose her deepest part, her most vulnerable heart, only to have you convolute in a paroxysm of self-possessed gratification, followed by your withdrawal into post-ejaculative relational non-interest?

Every time she sucks you into an uncontrollable need to ejaculate, she has conquered you. She controls you and masters you. She is in charge, sexually, no matter what manly gestures you make before ejaculating.

With a simple flick of her tongue, a silky moan, or a slurping tilt of her pelvis, she can drain you of life. And, deep down, she knows the world can do the same to you.

A superior man may choose to ejaculate occasionally. But such a choice is made freely, before even engaging in sex, not after it is too late, at the last uncontrollable moment before the physiological roller coaster starts heading down the deep dive into screaming release. A superior man is dedicated to the magnification of love through sexuality. He does not settle for less than the total surrender of his woman's heart, as well as his own, into the fullness of divine union. The pleasures of this dissolution into love so far exceed the typical genital spurt that ejaculation is easily bypassed or postponed once a man and woman have expanded their sexual capacity.

Just as your woman tests you emotionally, so she will test you sexually. Even when you are trying not to ejaculate, she may energetically begin to "pull" the ejaculation from you. As always, her deepest pleasure is in feeling your fullness, your strength, and your love, even while she is testing you. When you don't ejaculate, but demonstrate that the fullness of loving is more important to you than the quick thrill of genital release, then she can truly trust you. But she will continue to test your capacity for loving, even once you've demonstrated your capacity to bypass ejaculation for the sake of a much more profound bliss.

The bottom line is this: If ejaculation is not completely a matter of conscious choice for you, your woman knows she controls you sexually. And as long as she knows she's in charge, she won't trust you enough to relax fully in the force of your loving. She will always keep her heart somewhat protected. Rather than surrender so deeply in your embrace that she is splayed into divine brightness, she will go for whatever moist pleasures she can get before you lose interest.

Your woman will be sexually, emotionally, and spiritually unfulfilled to the extent that you are addicted to ejaculation. And, in many ways, the world will be just as unfulfilled by your gifts. Your addiction to cycles of release will stop you short of full and conscious dissolution in your deepest source, and so your true gifts will not emerge.

By strengthening your capacity for the fullest communion sexually, you also strengthen your capacity to dissolve into the source of life and re-emerge soaked in gifts, erect with purpose, and full of desire to give your deepest gifts in the face of worldly resistance to you. A superior man dissolves into the mystery and re-emerges full of love to give, again and again, without petering out, in his sexual relationship with his woman, and in his creative relationship with the world. ◆

45

Breathe Down
the Front

*All men tend to have blocks in the front of their body,
along an imaginary line that runs from the top of
the head, through the tongue, throat, heart, solar
plexus, navel, and genitals, down to the perineum.
The principal bodily key to mastering the world and
women is maintaining a full and open front of the
body at all times. The best method is through full and
relaxed breathing, drawing energy down the front,
and freeing attention from neurotic self-concern.*

When you get nervous, your stomach tightens. When you are sad-dened, a lump forms in your throat. When you are threatened, your solar plexus feels queasy. When you think hard, your forehead wrin-kles. When you consider the unsure future, you tense your jaw. For much of the day, you are tightening, tensing, and contracting the front of your body, from the top of your head, through your chest, and all the way down past your gut.

The front of your body, especially your belly, is the place where your energy meets the energy of the world. When the front of your body is open and relaxed, your power flows freely, and your presence fills the room. You've probably been with people who seem to occupy more space in the room than most people. They seem to command attention, even though they are not doing anything obvious to attract it. The front of their body is so open that their energy flows freely through the room, magnifying their presence.

Such people are remarkably relaxed, poised, and attentive. They are not all wrapped up in their own self-concern, hunched over a sunken chest, gritting their teeth, and hardly breathing. This is the picture of a closed belly and chest. If the front of your body has accumulated tension, throughout the day and throughout the years, you will hardly be able to sit up straight. Your belly and chest will be tight. Your thoughts will center on yourself. Your energy will remain constricted in your head and your awareness limited to self-concern. Your powerful presence won't fill the room at all. You might not even be noticed.

Right now, notice your breath. Are you inhaling so deeply you feel your genitals bulging slightly? Is your belly rising an falling with your inhale and exhale, like a mighty bellows? Your belly and lower abdomen are special places of power. If your breath does not reach these areas, you can't recharge your batteries. You will feel weak and unsure of yourself. Your effect in the world will be minimal, less than your full potential.

Inhale deeply, through your nose, and breathe through whatever tensions you notice in your body. Inhale deeply into your lower belly. Then exhale. On your next inhalation, breathe into your lower and upper belly. Then exhale. On your next inhalation, fill your entire belly, then your solar plexus and lower chest. Then exhale. Then inhale and fill your belly, solar plexus, and your entire chest, in that order. For several breaths, inhale fully in this way, filling your belly, solar plexus, and finally your chest. Then exhale fully, slowly, and smoothly.

Throughout the day, practice this kind of breathing in random moments. Pay special attention to any part of your body that seems particularly tense or closed. For instance, if the area around your navel seems tight, then inhale into that area. Literally inhale right into that area and open it with the force of your inhaled breath. Like filling a balloon, you can stretch open the entire front of your body with your inhale. In this way, you counter the effects of accumulated fear and anxiety stored in your body, which diminish your presence and force in the world. Throughout the day, as soon as you feel tension in the front of your body, inhale into that area and open it.

The main way you generate bodily tension is by turning your attention back on yourself in self-concern, curling into yourself so tightly you feel all knotted up. Therefore, the main cure is to give yourself to others. Whenever you notice that you are mulling over your own problems, knotting energy into your body as tension, take that energy and create a gift for others. It could be as simple as doing the dishes in the sink, or as complex as building a business that will benefit others. Convert into service the energy that is knotting up the front of your body. Your tension is only the energy of a gift that has become backed up, unexpressed, in your body.

Your breath is a primary expression of your personal energy. Therefore, your breath is one of the primary ways to give your gift to the world. You can use your breath to open other people's knots of tension, just as you open your own. Suppose you are with a person who seems a little tense. You can allow yourself to feel his tensions, and then inhale into his tensions, just as if they were yours. Inhale and open his tensions with the force of your inhalation. Then, exhale and release all tensions, yours and his. Inhale and open his knots with the force of your breath, then exhale and release all contraction, leaving only relaxation and love. All of this occurs without any physical contact. In fact, he probably won't have any idea that you are doing anything unusual whatsoever.

You could do this practice at work, with your lover, or with a whole crowd on a bus. If you are alone in your home, you could imagine all the tension in the world and inhale the force of life into this tension to open it up. Then exhale, releasing the tension into love to be dissolved, like a handful of salt released into the ocean. By practicing this form of breathing, you uncurl your attention from yourself, alleviating the knots of contraction in the front of your own body. And at the same time, you assume your true status as servant to others, who also, in their own way, are serving you.

These kinds of practices may seem odd to some people. But before you write such practices off as whimsical hokiness, try them. Do them, and find out the results for yourself. The next time you are in a meeting with others, inhale into the front of your body and open all the knots, letting your force expand out into the room as a blessing, feeling all stress dissolve in the ocean of love on your exhale. Feeling the unease of others, open their knots with the force of your inhale, and then let the knots dissolve with the release of your exhale. Pervade the room with your conscious loving in this way.

Even now, in this moment, inhale down into the front of your body, fully expanding your belly and opening your solar plexus and heart. Allow your fullness of force to expand outward, through the room and beyond the room, so as to pervade all others with the conscious force of your breath. Make love with the world in this way, all day, pervading and dissolving all unease. Feel the world against your body like a naked woman, vulnerable and alive, and allow the front of your body to press into and through the world's body, liberating the knots of accumulated pain.

Also, when sexually embracing your woman, use your breath to open her body and heart, in exactly the same way*. Fill her with the force of your loving, inhaling down through the front of her body as if it were yours, filling her genitals, belly, and heart with love energy. Then exhale, and let both of you dissolve in the ocean of your loving. Always pervade *through* her with your breath, inhaling and exhaling, so that her tension and closure dissolve in the force of your loving, and you dissolve in the giving. ◆

---

* For a book-length treatment of superior sexuality, see *The Enlightened Sex Manual*, by David Deida, Sounds True, 2004.

46

Ejaculate Up
the Spine

*For most men, ejaculation involves spewing their
energy and semen out through their genitals.
Afterward, they feel they have released stress. The
superior man's orgasm more often explodes up
his spine and into his brain, from there raining
down through his body like an ambrosial bliss
of rejuvenation. The technique for converting
depletive orgasms into rejuvenative orgasms involves
contracting the pelvic floor near the genitals and
drawing energy upward along the spine, though
the use of breath, feeling, and intention.*

What is premature ejaculation? Some men ejaculate before entering their woman's vagina. Others ejaculate after ten minutes
of sexual intercourse. What matters is not when you ejaculate, but how
deeply you are able to commune in love, with no boundaries, through the
form of sexual embrace. If your ejaculation signs the end to your session
of loving before both you and your woman have fully opened yourselves,
then your ejaculation is premature.

If you are like most men, your first sexual experiences as a teenager
involved masturbation. Masturbating over and over ends up conditioning
your body and nervous system to an habitual sequence: genital stimulation,

mental fantasy, building up tension, and ejaculating. Teenage masturbation is essentially an exercise in fantasy, done alone, without much love or even human intimacy. By the time most men are having sex with women, they repeat the same sequence they learned while masturbating. Sex has become a road toward ejaculation, a road paved with internal imagery, self-enclosure, and the desire to release tension.

To realize the full potential of sex, you must learn how to recondition your body and nervous system. You must learn how to unhabitualize the mechanics of your ejaculation, and convert your orgasm into a massive profusion of energy which deepens, not ends, the lovemaking session.

The first step is undoing the habits you learned while masturbating as a teenager. Instead of tensing your muscles as you become sexually stimulated, learn to relax them. When you notice your face squinching up, relax it. When you notice your breath getting fast and shallow, slow it down and deepen it. When you notice your belly tight and your chest hard, open your belly and soften the area around your heart.

The next step is to redirect your attention. Learn to feel your partner more than your own sensations during sex. Rather than curling attention into yourself and feeling the pleasures moving in your own body, feel outward, into, and through your partner. Feel your partner more than you feel yourself. Feel her movement, her moans, and her internal energy.

Eventually, with practice, you will be able to feel through your partner, as if your partner's body were a doorway into a vast open space of energy, light, and awareness. This unobstructed feeling is the basis for true lovemaking. Extend your love out beyond yourself and, in time, through and beyond your woman. This takes practice, since there is a strong tendency to focus on your own physical sensations, especially during times of intense sexual stimulation. Counteract this tendency by practicing to feel beyond yourself and through your partner as if there were no obstructions to your loving at all.

Besides relaxing and loving into and through your partner, you must become very sensitive to the force of your breath. Breath moves life energy through your body as well as your partner's. If your breathing becomes too shallow, the life force cannot be conducted through your body. Instead, this force builds up, usually in your head or in your genitals. If it builds in your head, you will begin to spend more and more time fantasizing about sex and women. It if builds up in your genitals, you will feel the need to ejaculate, either through sex or masturbation.

Therefore, if you have not breathed fully during the day, by the time you approach your sexual partner you will be filled with fantasies and ejaculative urge. So, a large part of avoiding premature ejaculation is to breathe fully, deeply, and with great force, throughout the day. Your inhales should feel like they are drawing energy down the front of your body, filling your belly and genital region. Your exhales should feel like they are moving energy from your pelvic floor, up your spine, into your head.

By breathing fully in this circle, down your front and up your spine, your internal energy can flow freely. Your head and genitals don't get clogged or tense with energy. And your urge to ejaculate is diminished.

Sex intensifies the life force in your body. As you become more and more stimulated, your breath quickens and your body begins to writhe with energy, which tends to become focused in the genital region. Unless you are careful to move this energy with your breath, it will build up in your genitals and cause a pressure that wants to be released through ejaculation.

There is a specific exercise you can perform throughout sex and also during the approach to orgasm. By doing this exercise you will convert the direction of the orgasm, so instead of ejaculating out your penis, you will "ejaculate" up your spine, experiencing intense bodily bliss and emotional openness, far beyond the quick pleasure and depleted peace following an ejaculative orgasm.

To practice this exercise, you must learn to consciously contract the muscles of the floor of your pelvis. This area includes your genitals, anus, and perineum, which is the space between your anus and genitals. This exercise of contracting your pelvic floor feels a lot like you are trying to stop yourself from going to the bathroom.

In addition to contracting the floor of your pelvis, practice pulling it upward into your body and toward your spine. This upward pull will actually lift your scrotum slightly up toward your body.

As a single movement, practice contracting and pulling upward the entire floor of your pelvis, including the anus, perineum, and genitals. You can practice this in sets of 15 or 20 contractions, holding them as long as you can. Do several sets like this, three or four times a day.

Eventually, you will be able to contract and pull up your pelvic floor easily, holding it for as long as you want. This means you have developed the necessary muscular control. Now you can practice the more subtle work of moving the energy up your spine.

At first, it may seem like you are just imagining internal energy moving in your body. But, with practice, you will more easily see or feel this energy moving. After all, it is the same energy that, during intense sexual stimulation, you have no trouble feeling build up in your genital region, which is then released through ejaculation. You can feel it building up like water behind a dam, wanting to burst out. Well, the same energy can burst upward. And when it does, you will experience an orgasm far more pleasurable than the brief burst of a typical genital ejaculation, and also far more healing and enlivening.

While you are having sex, but before you are close to ejaculating, practice contracting your pelvic floor as just discussed. While you contract it and pull upward, breathe the energy up your spine. You will have to experiment to determine whether to inhale or to exhale the energy up your spine, although most people find that exhaling up the spine works best. If you combine the upward contraction of your pelvic floor with breathing up your spine, you should lose just a little bit of your erection as well as the need to ejaculate. As you continue making love, repeat this exercise as often as you need to in order to maintain relaxation and openness.

Even while practicing this technique, you may notice that you occasionally come very close to having an orgasm. At this point, stop moving, apply the upward contraction of your pelvic floor, and breathe the orgasm energy up your spine. In addition to the upward contraction of your pelvic floor while breathing up the spine, some men find it helpful to clench their fists and teeth while looking upward with their eyes, especially when the urge toward ejaculation is particularly strong. With practice, however, all the muscular action becomes very subtle and gentle, until the entire exercise is done primarily through your breath, feeling, and intention.

When the energy shoots up your spine, relax and enjoy the colors, feelings, and blisses that will fill your head and rain down through your body. Once you are proficient at this exercise, you can evoke the same sensations in your partner by feeling into your partner from your heart as the orgasm shoots up your spine. The upward movement of your energy will magnetize the same movement in hers.

These practices will not be successful unless you are able to surrender as love in the midst of sexual embrace. Love is the governor of energy. More and more, you must practice being love in the form of sexual coupling. Regardless of how tough your day has been, regardless of the burdens you face in your life, sexing should be a time of practicing love. Like meditation or prayer, sex should be a special time of practicing opening your heart and giving love fully, into and through your partner, and in communion with that which you hold most sacred.

If your heart is closed, your energy will be obstructed, and you will never be able to convert your spurt to a lightning bolt of love. If you don't practice love, your sexual energy will be governed by old habits of body and emotion, which are all about the tiny commotion of ejaculation. So, if you want to expand sexual bliss as fully as possible, remember that your emotional disposition is far more important than the technical exercises themselves.

Because each individual is different, you must experiment and discover which techniques, done as exercises of love, work best for you. With practice, you will easily be able to experience deep non-ejaculatory orgasms that shoot up your body as light, leaving your heart wide open, your energy enlivened, and your body reverberating in bliss. You will be able to make love for as long as you want, and sex will rejuvenate, rather than deplete, your life force.

In summary, this is what to remember as you experiment and discover which techniques work best for you:

1. Rather than fantasizing or entertaining inward sexual imagery of any kind, remain totally present, aware of your own body, breath, and mind, and especially attentive to your partner. Break the masturbatory habit of inward fantasy by consciously practicing sex as a relational play of love with your partner.

2. Keep your body and breath relaxed and full. Especially keep the front of your body relaxed, so that your belly is vast and your heart is soft and wide. This will help prevent too much tension from accumulating in any one area.

3. Learn to feel into, and then through, your partner, so that your attention is directed beyond your own sensations and even beyond your partner's sensations. Practice feeling outward, without limit, as if you were feeling to infinity. In other words, whatever you are feeling, feel it fully, and then feel through and beyond it, so that sex becomes a constant feeling through and beyond every sensation, rather than focusing on any particular sensation.

4. Throughout the day and during the sexual session, practice breathing so that your inhalation moves energy down the front of your

body and the exhalation moves energy up your spine. Excessive, chronic thinking or addiction to ejaculation is often a sign that your energy is blocked and you are not yet breathing fully in this circle throughout the day.

5. During sex, occasionally practice the upward contraction of the floor of your pelvis while breathing sexual energy up your spine, so it fills your whole body. Especially as you begin to approach orgasm, you can combine the upward contraction of your pelvic floor with breathing up the spine in order to shoot your orgasm up into your brain, and even out through the top of your head, rather than down and out your genitals. This upward orgasm will then feel like it is gently seeping down through every cell of your body, saturating you with thick open light.

These techniques will be less than effective unless you practice love during sex. The natural intelligence of love itself acts to circulate energy in the most healthy way possible. These techniques are mostly exercises to counteract years of poor sexual habits, usually initiated during teenage masturbation. After eliminating the mechanical habit of ejaculation and unobstructing your energy, the force of your heart will very naturally guide your orgasm so it explodes upward, throughout the body and brain, before raining down in a profusion of bliss, which not only rejuvenates you, but dissolves your edges like shadows in the sun. ◆

PART

EIGHT

Men's and Women's
Yoga of Intimacy

47

Take into Account
the Primary Asymmetry

Intimate relationship is never the priority in a masculine man's life and always the priority in a feminine woman's life. If a man has a masculine sexual essence, then his priority is his mission, his direction toward greater release, freedom, and consciousness. If a woman has a feminine sexual essence, then her priority is the flow of love in her life, including her relationship with a man whom she can totally trust, in body, emotion, mind, and spirit. Man and woman must support each other in their priorities if the relationship is going to serve them both.

Although you and your woman are equal beings, you are very different creatures. If she has a feminine sexual essence, her core will be fulfilled when love is flowing. For example, she can experience difficulties in her career, but if full love is flowing in her life—with her children, friends, and with you—then her core will be fulfilled.

Not so for you. If you have a masculine sexual essence, then your woman and children can be loving you all day and night, but if your career or mission is obstructed, you will not feel at ease. You won't even *want* to share much intimate time with your woman until you have your career or mission back on track.

Your woman's core is fulfilled by love. Your core is released from stress by aligning your life with your mission. To you, intimacy is something to be enjoyed in addition to your purpose. To your woman, intimacy is at the core of her life, and the tone of your intimacy colors everything else she does.

When your intimacy is going great, your woman's life is filled with the color of love. She feels good at work, at home, in bed. When the intimacy is not going so great, when your woman feels unloved, rejected, hurt, or abandoned by you, then her day will be colored by hurt. At work, at home, and in the bed, the pain of unlove will color her disposition.

But, for you, things are different. When your intimacy is going bad, you can't wait to leave the house and go to work; there, you can be in your element, aligned with your purpose, and happy. For you, the intimacy is just one aspect of your life. When you are absorbed in your mission, you often forget entirely about your intimacy. For your woman, the intimacy is at the core of her life and colors everything else she does. This is the primary asymmetry in intimacy.

It goes much farther than this, though. For most men, their woman is replaceable. Harsh, but true. If you are like most men, you know, deep down, that if you were to lose your present woman, you would deeply grieve, but you could eventually find another. Many times, in fact, you have probably fantasized about finding another woman even before you lose the one you have. Because a man's priority is his mission, he will always gravitate to a woman whom he feels would most support his mission. If he feels another woman would enliven him and give him more energy for his work, he might desire her as an intimate partner.

However, you are lodged in the heart of your woman. She feels you all day. She senses where you are at. Feeling-threads from her heart are connected to your heart, day and night. You are not replaceable in her perception. She does not frequently consider other options, as you probably do. Whereas you live in a world of relational possibility, she lives in a world of relational actuality. Your relationship with her is not only at the core of her life, but is also the main determinant of her mood.

If your woman has rejected her own feminine core, then she will struggle against her inherent heart-connection with you. She will try to identify with her masculine side, attempting to de-prioritize you and your relationship. She will think that she must "live her own life" and put more energy into her own career, for instance. While it is obviously healthy for every man and woman to learn to become whole and independent, it is self-destructive for your woman to try to lessen the import of your relationship in her life. If she has a feminine sexual essence, the desire for the flow of love is at her core, no matter how dedicated she is to her career or other activities.

Without a deep and loving intimacy—with you or with the divine— she hurts. It will never work for her to try to quell the pain by absorbing herself in her career, her art, or her friends. If she has a feminine essence, she must honor herself by owning her deep desire for the flow of love in her heart, just as a person with a masculine essence must honor his or her direction in order to be truly happy. Our culture has become so anti-feminine that many women are trying to deny their feminine core desires and adopt the masculine way of dedication to mission. By denying their feminine essence, such women are predisposing themselves to emptiness of heart, depression, and bodily symptoms of disease.

Likewise, you must not deny your woman's feminine essence by feeling or saying to her, "Your whole life seems to revolve around our relationship! That's not healthy. You should have your own life, your own direction, your own career and friends. Stop complaining about our intimate prob-lems and get a life!"

While it is common sense that she should live a fulfilling and engaging life outside of your relationship, it is sexual wisdom to understand that her feminine essence will always hold the flow of love at its center. That's just the way it is. This flow of love could be in direct relationship with the divine, although it is usually in relationship with a man.

The desire for intimate loving is as central to your woman's life as the mission toward freedom—financial, psychological, and spiritual—is to yours. Think of how many hours a day you dedicate to your mission and compare that with how many hours a day you spend serving your woman's deep desire for the magnification of love. If you want her to honor and support you in your quest for freedom, you must honor and support her in her love of loving. Her devotion to love has a lot to teach you.

Some men feel guilty for not being as "into" the relationship as their woman is. You must understand that this is natural. If you have a masculine essence and your woman has a feminine essence, you will never be as concerned, distraught, or elated about your intimacy as your woman is. Don't fake it. Don't try to act concerned for the sake of your woman. She can feel where you are really at. Instead, be authentic to your core desires, and dedicate your life, with utter impeccability, to your highest goals.

If one of your highest goals is psychological or spiritual freedom, then you will highly value your intimacy. Nobody will press your buttons or reflect your asshole to you better than your woman. She will point out your weaknesses better than a boot camp drill sergeant. She will reflect your ambiguity or clarity better than any workshop teacher. She will do you better than a whore and give you more loving than you can handle. And all the while she will shower your life with radiant blessing, healing, and enlivenment—if she learns to own her true feminine desires and you learn to own your true masculine desires.

When you both honor the primary asymmetry in intimacy, you can each concentrate on your true desires rather than compromising for the sake of an imaginary truce between genders. When your life is truly aligned with your highest purpose, you will become more present, more loving, and more humorous. Your woman will then be the first recipient of your magnified presence, love, and humor. If your intimacy is not constantly growing in this way, your life is not aligned with your highest purpose.

Likewise, if your woman devotes herself to her true heart desires, you will feel it. Her energy, radiance, wisdom, and power to create heaven on earth will feed you constantly—even when it is not directed toward you. You will be inspired by her magic, enchanted by her sexuality, awed by her knowingness, and enlivened by the life that flows so lovingly through her body. However, if she has chosen to deny her heart desire and adopt more masculine goals of purpose and mission as her core needs, both of you will suffer. Her radiance will diminish, her guardedness will increase, and neither of your hearts will feel relaxed in the intimacy.

Your woman could be a corporate executive and you could be a househusband. That's fine, as long as you are living your highest purpose and her life is devoted to love. Honor this primary asymmetry, in yourself and in your woman. Only when you are willing to support each other's core desires will the intimacy give each of you what you want, and then perhaps bring you beyond even that, into the utter joy of being, of which your relationship is only a hope. ◆

48

You Are Responsible
for the Growth in Intimacy

*There are masculine and feminine gifts in intimacy,
and each gift comes with its own responsibility.
The direction of growth of a relationship is primarily
the man's responsibility. The energy of an intimacy—
pleasure, sexual flow, and vitality—is primarily the
woman's responsibility. A simplified way of saying this
is that the man is responsible for the woman's depth of
love, or openness of mood, and the woman is responsible
for the man's "erection" or energy in the body.*

Once you have grown into independent adulthood, you no longer need somebody to take care of you. You can be responsible for yourself. In particular, you realize that you are responsible for your own happiness. Nobody can live your life for you. You must create your own health, success, and happiness.

This sense of self-responsibility is only a partial maturity, however. Beyond self-responsibility lies the responsibility to give your gift. It is important to grow beyond dependence on your intimate partner for your own happiness. But it's equally important to grow beyond simple independence and autonomy. The next stage of intimacy after personal independence has been attained is the mutual flow of gifting, or serving each other in love.

You may have noticed that your woman can get lost in her moods. She can get on a roll of hyper-nervousness. Or, she can feel dejected and mope around the house surrounded by a black cloud. It is extremely difficult for most women to get out of their mood once they are in it. Your loving intervention is one of your great masculine gifts. The point is not to be her therapist, but to be her wake-up call, her heart-opener, her reminder of the primacy of love. If it takes you more than five minutes to open her into love, you are probably talking too much and acting too little. Or, perhaps you have forgotten your true purpose.

Your masculine gift is to know where you are, where you want to be, and what you need to do to get there. If you don't know one of these, then you need to discover it by any means necessary. This vision is, essentially, the basic gift you have to offer your woman, as well as the world. If you have no higher vision than the day-to-day grind of housework, job, childcare, TV, and vacations, you are failing your birthright. Your woman will feel cheated and ungifted by you, as will the world. And they will both give you less of their gifts in return.

If your woman is always stressed out, you need to know what she could do with her life, in very practical terms, so she can relax. Perhaps she needs to exercise more, meditate more, change her career, dance more, or spend more time with her women friends. If your woman feels unfulfilled most of the time, you need to know what she is missing. How often does she open her heart and body in the irrepressible ecstasy of devotional surrender? How often does she abandon herself fully into the divine love which surrounds her? How often do you serve her to do so?

Are you playing the game of "sensitive man," giving her "space" to be miserable rather than offering her your consistent and fearless gifting? And if she doesn't want your gift, your deepest wisdom and unsuppressed loving, then why would you want to be with her? Your main gift in intimacy is to guide her, moment by moment, out of her moods and into the openness of loving. And then, day by day, to guide her life into greater degrees of divine love, even beyond the relationship, so that her life becomes primarily communion, gifting, and celebration. If you cannot offer your woman such guidance, what can you offer her? Why is she with you? What is your relationship all about?

To offer this masculine gift, you must cultivate your sense of daily practice. Like a musician practicing his art, you must practice, daily, the art of feeling through your fear, feeling to your edge, and then living just beyond your edge, neither slinking into private consolation nor pushing so hard you disconnect from your source. The source that is your deepest truth must become more and more the impulse of your life. Over time, all of your activities must become aligned to this source. And so must your relationship.

Because you probably tend to become lost in your thoughts, in your goals, and in your projects, one of the main gifts your woman can offer you is getting you into your body, into the present, into love, which connects you to your source. Through her touch, her loving, and her attractiveness, she can also give you energy, so that your whole body becomes like an erection, full and alive, and ready to penetrate the world into love. Your woman might be the President of the United States. Still, if you have a masculine sexual essence, her special gift to you is to bring you back into your body with the attractive force of her feminine energy.

Without a woman to serve your present embodiment of love, you might spend most of your time working on your projects, staring into a computer screen, churning thoughts in your head, or seeking future goals of financial or spiritual freedom. Meanwhile, you have lost touch with the present, with your body and your woman.

When you can simply be with your body and your woman, fully present, without pulling away into your head of separation, then the boundaries begin to dissolve in the openness of your loving. When you can feel through your woman and your body, they become as if transparent, and the source and radiant substance of existence becomes obvious through them. Your natural gesture in this revelation of transparency is service. There is nothing to do but dissolve in the giving of your gift.

Your woman may not want to receive your gift. Your woman may resist your gift. And so may the world. But you have no choice. Live at your edge. Love as fully as possible. Let your body be erect with the energy of your deep source. And take full responsibility for giving whatever love you have realized to the world and your woman. Both will seem to refuse you and seduce you, until you can feel through them.

Feel through your woman and the world, and die in the giving of your gift. ◆

49

Insist on Practice and Growth

Direction in life is a masculine priority, even in intimate relationship. A less spiritually mature man may say to his woman, "My way or the highway!" A man in the process of growing will often soften his direction and seek a compromise with his woman, playing Mr. Nice Guy. But a superior man will not settle for less than the fullest incarnation of love of which he and his woman are capable. With compassion, he slices through all bullshit and demands authenticity and humor. It's as if he were saying to his woman, "The divine way or the highway!" It's the same masculine insistence on direction that a weaker man will demand. But rather than wanting his woman to follow his personal direction, a superior man wants her to move in the direction that most serves her growth in love and happiness. He will settle for nothing less.

I f you don't know your own direction in life, you certainly will stand on shaky ground offering your woman direction. So the first step is to align your own life so that, at least in this present moment, you are living at your edge, fully aligned with your sense of purpose. If you are not absolutely certain that, in this moment, you are living exactly the life you need to, then your woman will feel your lack of clarity, and she will fight any kind of guidance you offer her.

You will tend to forget the purpose of your existence as you get lost in your daily round of projects, business, and duties. Your woman will tend to forget the love at her core as she gets lost in cycles of mood and emotion. As a gift to both of you, you must cut through your own nose-to-the-grindstone mentality as well as your woman's ensconcement in sadness, fear, and anger, and reveal the truth. However deeply you have penetrated into the mystery of existence, it is that depth from which your gift will spring. Any obstruction to that depth, by yourself or your woman, must be cut through, in the present moment, so your gift may come from the deepest source.

If you don't cut through and take direction, your woman will. Masculine and feminine energies in intimacy are governed by the law of conservation. The less masculine direction you are living in truth, the more masculine direction your woman will take on. If you are lolling about in bozoland, or working hard but actually not living your true gift, then your woman will resent your lack of deep direction. She will begin to take on the masculine blade herself, trying to cut through your lolling, so that you feel the urgency, connect to your depth, and really give your gift.

Since at your core, however, you are masculine, her masculine attempt to cut through your lolling will depolarize you. You will bash heads with her, like two rams, since both of you are in your masculine. And if you move into your feminine, things may get worse. A deep habit may develop wherein no matter how strong you are in the business world, you become pussywhipped in your relationship. Your woman gets sharp and masculine, you become falsely receptive and agreeable, and meanwhile both of you feel like vomiting.

If your woman is chronically sharp with you, it is most likely a sign that, regardless of how successful you are outside of your intimacy, you are not aligning both of your lives with the highest truth. You are not cutting through the underbrush of your duties and your woman's moods to reveal the fertile ground source of your lives. And so your woman must wield her own sword. By the law of conservation of masculine and feminine energy, whatever masculine gifts you aren't offering, your woman will naturally try to offer. But since, in truth, your core is masculine, her masculine offerings will most likely turn you off, eventually even repulsing you.

You are entirely responsible for cutting through your own laziness, addictions, and unclarity. There is nothing to wait for and nobody to blame. Whatever techniques are appropriate, use them. Try talking with your friends, using therapy, practicing meditation or prayer, going on a vision quest, reading scripture, walking in nature, keeping a journal, or studying with a teacher. Remember that your success with any method you choose depends entirely on your actual commitment to discovering your deepest truth and aligning your life with it.

You could meditate until you're blue in the face, but it won't work, if, when it comes down to it, you'd rather masturbate, read the newspaper, or watch TV than cut through your addictions, discipline your daily life, and give your gift from your deepest, most blissful source. The quality of your intent and the consistency and depth of your application determine the results of your direction in gifting—as well as your capacity to guide your woman's life into greater happiness and bodily surrender into love. ◆

Restore Your Purpose in
Solitude and with Other Men

*A man rediscovers and fine tunes his purpose
in solitude, in challenging situations, and in the
company of other men who won't settle for his
bullshit. But women strengthen their feminine
radiance best in the company of other women in
mutual celebration and play. A man must arrange for
both forms of restoration: his own solitude and men's
gatherings, and his woman's time with other women.*

▼

I f you spend too much time with your woman, you will rub off on each
other in the worst way. In order to get along together, she will begin to
adopt your masculine patterns of speech, denying her feminine desire to
flow in play and pleasure without having to make masculine-style sense
or fulfill a purpose. You will begin to adopt her feminine patterns of
touch and affection, denying your desire to get down to it, with your mission or your woman. Instead, you will find yourself pecking your woman
on the cheek or giving her hugs and pats of lovey-dovey reassurance. In
short, the goddess and the warrior will become neutralized householders
sharing only the mildest play of sexual polarity.

In order to enliven her feminine core, your woman should spend
time every day in absolute abandon and celebration. During these times
of dancing, singing, laughter, and sheer delight, her body and mind
should be totally released of any obligation to be masculine—directed,

controlled, structured, or goal-oriented. These occasions are most rejuvenating when she is with other women, magnifying and rejoicing in each others' feminine radiance and flow. If your woman lacks this frequent feminine rejuvenation, she will develop symptoms of depressed feminine energy: disease (especially in her more feminine parts), lack of life energy, low sexual desire and enjoyment, and a blue, downhearted, despondent disposition.

Much of the modern men's movement has concentrated on men reclaiming their inner feminine energy. If you want to revitalize your own feminine energy, then you can do pretty much the same as women do to revitalize their feminine energy. You can go out into the woods and sing and dance and laugh with your friends. For men who have become rigidly stuck in their masculine direction, without allowing the flow of joy and sharing in their lives, this is good medicine.

But for men who have lost their sense of purpose, who don't know what their life is about, or who have trouble aligning their life with their truth, singing and dancing aren't the remedy. The cure for lack of purpose is to be challenged to live at your edge, since you have lost the capacity to live there by yourself.

The two ways to bring you right to your masculine edge of power are austerity and challenge.

Austerity means to eliminate the comforts and cushions in your life that you have learned to snuggle into and lose wakefulness. Take away anything that dulls your edge. No newspapers or magazines. No TV. No candy, cookies, or sweets. No sex. No cuddling. No reading of anything at all while you eat or sit on the toilet. Reduce working time to a necessary minimum. No movies. No conversation that isn't about truth, love, or the divine.

If you take on these disciplines for a few weeks, as well as any other disciplines that may particularly cut through your unique habits of dullness, then your life will be stripped of routine distraction. All that will be left is the edge you have been avoiding by means of your daily routine.

You will have to face the basic discomfort and dissatisfaction that is the hidden texture of your life. You will be alive with the challenge of living your truth, rather than hiding from it.

Unadorned suffering is the bedmate of masculine growth. Only by staying intimate with your personal suffering can you feel through it to its source. By putting all your attention into work, TV, sex, and reading, your suffering remains unpenetrated, and the source remains hidden. Your life becomes structured entirely by your favorite means of sidestepping the suffering you rarely allow yourself to feel. And when you do touch the surface of your suffering, perhaps in the form of boredom, you quickly pick up a magazine or the remote control.

Instead, feel your suffering, rest with it, embrace it, make love with it. Feel your suffering so deeply and thoroughly that you penetrate it, and realize its fearful foundation. Almost everything you do, you do because you are afraid to die. And yet dying is exactly what you are doing, from the moment you are born. Two hours of absorption in a good Super Bowl telecast may distract you temporarily, but the fact remains. You were born as a sacrifice. And you can either participate in the sacrifice, dissolving in the giving of your gift, or you can resist it, which is your suffering.

By eliminating the safety net of comforts in your life, you have the opportunity to free fall in this moment between birth and death, right through the hole of your fear, into the unthreatenable openness which is the source of your gifts. The superior man lives as this spontaneous sacrifice of love.

The other means, besides austerity, for rediscovering your masculine core is through challenge. The more superficial forms of challenge include activities like mountain climbing, ropes courses, competitive sports, and boot camp. These forms of physical challenge instantly enliven the masculine sense of purpose and direction, in men and women.

Deeper forms of challenge involve directly giving your gift in ways that have been blocked by your fear. If you have always been afraid of public speaking, you can take on the challenge of speaking in public once a week for three months. If you fail and miss an appointment one week, the following week you must give three talks. If you have always wanted to write a novel, but could never finish one, you tell your friends that you are going to complete one chapter a week (or a month) for the next year. Every time you don't complete your weekly goal, you owe your friends $100. If you don't complete your yearly goal, you owe them $10,000.

The point is, there must be a consequence for freezing in the face of fear. There are obvious consequences for freezing in the face of fear when mountain climbing or playing competitive sports. You must instill consequences throughout the rest of your life, unless you want to cling to the safety net of superficial pleasures.

The most potent forms of masculine realignment involve both austerity and challenge. Go to the middle of the woods, by yourself, with only survival necessities. Nothing to read, nothing to do. Fast from food and don't sleep for as long as possible. Challenge your attention with some practice, like chanting or ritual movement, so that your attention doesn't drift or become balmy. Open yourself and wait. Do not cover your suffering. Do not quit before you fall through the hole of your fear and emerge with a vision of your true mission, the unique form of your living sacrifice.

This kind of isolation and challenge is an extreme and potent form of masculine vision questing, but there are more common forms that are useful in everyday life. Spend time every day in solitude, with no distractions. Just sit, for ten minutes. No fidgeting, no channel surfing, no magazine thumbing. Just be, exactly as you are, not trying to change anything. Stay with your suffering, until you fall through it and intuit the groundless source of your life.

Just as your woman must regularly spend time with only women, you must regularly spend time with only men. At least once a week, get together with your men friends to serve one another. Cut through the bullshit and talk with each other straight. If you feel your friend is wasting his life, tell him so, because you love him. Welcome such criticism from your friends. Suggest challenges for each other to take on, in order to bring each other through the fears which limit your surrender in gifting. Always agree on consequences for not persisting in the challenge. For instance, if you agree to ravish your wife for three hours every other day for a week, then also agree to mow your friend's yard if you miss a day of ravishment.

You should alternate these kinds of "cutting through the bullshit" gatherings with masculine celebrations. Even during these celebrations, though, there should be a challenge to remain conscious and undistracted. They are not occasions for lapsing from fullness, but for communing beyond fear. Perhaps you can all go swimming in ice cold water together. Or drink to the point of inebriation and then spend the rest of the night chanting hymns of the mystery of existence—nobody allowed to drift. Whatever you do, share as much loving as you can with your friends, without settling for mediocrity or less than each man's fullest gift.

Make sure that you arrange for your woman's rejuvenative time and your own. Otherwise, you will rot in the cushions of bargained stagnation and sexual neutralization which pad your true edge of living your gift in relationship. ◆

51

Practice
Dissolving

Like dissolving in the intensity of an orgasm,
a man's greatest desire is to be utterly released.

Moment by moment, practice loving through your woman and the world, allowing the force of your surrender to transform every moment into an orgasm of divine dissolution. Embrace every moment of experience as a lover, and trust whatever direction love moves you. Die in the giving of your gift, so you don't even notice you have stopped holding onto yourself. Fear is your final excuse. Don't fight it. Love through it. ◆

Titles by David Deida

Dear Lover

A Woman's Guide to Men, Sex, and Love's Deepest Bliss

How do you attract and keep a man capable of meeting what you most passionately yearn for? To answer this question, David Deida explores every aspect of the feminine practice of spiritual intimacy, from sexuality and lovemaking to family and career to emotions, trust, and commitment.

ISBN: 978-1-59179-260-4 / U.S. $16.95

Blue Truth

A Spiritual Guide to Life & Death and Love & Sex

David Deida presents a treasury of skills and insights for uncovering and offering your true heart of purpose, passion, and unquenchable love.

ISBN: 978-1-59179-259-8 / U.S. $16.95

Intimate Communion

Awakening Your Sexual Essence

David Deida's first book lays the foundation for his teaching on the integration of intimacy and authentic spiritual practice.

Finding God Through Sex

Awakening the One of Spirit Through the Two of Flesh

No matter how much we pray or meditate, it's not always easy to integrate sexual pleasure and spiritual depth. David Deida helps single men and women and couples of every orientation turn sex into an erotic act of deep devotional surrender.

ISBN: 978-1-59179-273-4 / U.S. $16.95

Wild Nights

Conversations with Mykonos about Passionate Love, Extraordinary Sex, and How to Open to God

Meet Mykonos—scurrilous madman and speaker of truth. A recollection of a unique relationship between a student and an extraordinary spiritual teacher.

ISBN: 978-1-59179-233-8 / U.S. $15.95

The Enlightened Sex Manual
Sexual Skills for the Superior Lover

The secret to enlightenment and great sex is revealed to be one and the same in this groundbreaking manual for adventurous lovers. The ultimate collection of skills for opening to the physical, emotional, and spiritual rewards of intimate embrace.

ISBN: 978-1-59179-585-8 / U.S. $15.95

It's a Guy Thing
An Owner's Manual for Women

David Deida answers more than 150 of women's most-asked questions about men and intimacy.

Instant Enlightenment
Fast, Deep, and Sexy

David Deida offers a wealth of priceless exercises and insights to bring "instant enlightenment" to the areas we need it most.

ISBN: 978-1-59179-560-5 / U.S. $12.95

AUDIO

Enlightened Sex
Finding Freedom & Fullness Through Sexual Union

A complete six-CD program to learn the secrets to transforming lovemaking into a spiritual gift to yourself, your lover, and the world.

ISBN: 978-1-59179-083-9 / U.S. $69.95

The Teaching Sessions:
The Way of the Superior Man
Revolutionary Tools and Essential Exercises for Mastering the Challenges of Women, Work, and Sexual Desire

A spiritual guide for today's man in search of the secrets to success in career, purpose, and sexual intimacy—now available on four CDs in this original author expansion of and companion to the bestselling book.

ISBN: 978-1-59179-343-4 / U.S. $29.95

For information about all of David Deida's books and audios, visit **www.deida.info.**

To place an order or to receive a free catalog of wisdom teachings for the inner life, visit **soundstrue.com**, call toll-free **800-333-9185**, or write: The Sounds True Catalog, PO Box 8010, Boulder, CO 80306.

About the Author

▼

Acknowledged as one of the world's most insightful and provocative teachers of our time, bestselling author David Deida continues to revolutionize the way that men and women grow spiritually and sexually. His teaching and writing on a radically practical spirituality for our time have been hailed as among the most original and authentic contributions to personal and spiritual growth currently available.

Known internationally for his unique workshops on spiritual growth and sacred intimacy, Deida has designed and developed a remarkably effective program of transformative practices that fully addresses spiritual awakening in mind, body, and heart. He is a founding associate of Integral Institute and has taught and conducted research at the University of California's Medical School in San Diego, University of California–Santa Cruz, San Jose State University, Lexington Institute in Boston, and Ecole Polytechnique in Paris, France.

Deida is known worldwide as the author of hundreds of essays, audios, books, videos, and articles that bring to light a fully integral approach to spirituality. His books are published in more than twenty-five languages worldwide and are required reading in university, church, and spiritual-center courses. They're also used as source texts in men's and women's groups around the world and are considered among the deepest resources for real spiritual transformation available. His recent books include *Blue Truth*, *The Enlightened Sex Manual*, and *Instant Enlightenment*.

For more information about David Deida's books, audios, videos, and teaching schedule, please visit **www.deida.info.**

About Sounds True

S ounds True was founded in 1985 with a clear vision: to disseminate spiritual wisdom. Located in Boulder, Colorado, Sounds True publishes teaching programs that are designed to educate, uplift, and inspire. We work with many of the leading spiritual teachers, thinkers, healers, and visionary artists of our time.

For a free catalog, or for more information on audio programs by David Deida, please visit soundstrue.com, call toll free at 800-333-9185, or write to us at the address below.

The Sounds True Catalog
PO Box 8010
Boulder CO 80306